D0616501

Christ-
Centered
Self-Esteem

Christ-Centered Self-Esteem

Seeing Ourselves Through God's Eyes

Charles R. Gerber

 COLLEGE PRESS
PUBLISHING COMPANY
Joplin, Missouri

Second Printing 1998
Printed and Bound in the United States of America
All Rights Reserved

Library of Congress Cataloging-in-Publication Data

Gerber, Charles R. (Charles Richard), 1958–
   Christ-centered self-esteem: seeing ourselves through God's
eyes / Charles R. Gerber.
     p.   cm.
   Includes bibliographical references.
   ISBN 0-89900-764-3
   1. Self-esteem–Religious aspects–Christianity.   I. Title.
BV4598.24.G47 1996
248.4–dc20   96-33525
                                                   CIP

Acknowledgments

Many people have helped in the writing of this book. There have been many people who have encouraged me during this project. This book is dedicated to my wife, Janelle. She has heard me speak on this topic for many years. She has put up with the late nights and hours of research.

To the staff at Christ In Youth in Joplin, Missouri: I want to thank you for the dedication you have shown to me. Thank you all for the love, support and encouragement you have given me through the years. You have allowed me to speak on this topic and many others during the past several years. You are friends and family to my wife, my two kids and me. Thank you for helping me teach "Christ-Centered Self-Esteem" across the nation. Without you I don't know if this project would have been completed.

FOREWORD

Almost all youth workers agree that "self-esteem" is a key determiner in the maturation process for adolescents. Almost all young people in trouble with the law suffer from low self-esteem as do most who never reach the courts but constitute the groups referred to by statistics quoted by educators, politicians, clergy, parents, policemen and media commentators.

The central question continues to be, "What will we do about it?" Obviously, each individual has his or her own particular set of circumstances and causes; however, social scientists look for solutions in environmental and cultural dysfunctions, politicians suggest structured or economic redress and psychologists attempt to adjust the attitudes and values of teenagers to fit the prevailing moral climate. All fall short of a lasting answer, and they leave out the spiritual dimension. Daniel Patrick Moynihan describes this dilemma accurately in his classic treatment, "Defining Deviancy Down."

On a personal level, I am suspicious of Christian writers who deny the findings of sociologists, psychologists, educators, and even politicians. The problems of youth and how they view themselves is a complex, multifaceted subject and all can offer insight. For people who believe in God, particularly Christians, it is equally foolish to ignore the Bible and what God, the Creator of us all, has revealed to us about ourselves and our world.

Charles Gerber has done an excellent job of bringing the Christian gospel to bear on the subject of self-esteem without yielding to the temptation to ignore the social sciences or to tear us away from the Bible toward the therapeutic model.

Christ-Centered Self-Esteem is what it says it is. It is a thoroughly researched and carefully written attempt to help us see that "self-esteem" is not a psychological buzzword but a necessary part of our God-given humanity. He helps us to see that the attack of our souls' enemy is well directed toward the self because it is in this strategic assault toward our souls that the effectiveness of our lives can be lost. Gerber helps us to understand that God is not the enemy of the "self" but of "selfishness," not even of the ego but of egotism. To a large degree this constitutes the battle between psychology and Christianity. This book lowers the suspicion and turns on new lights. All those who care about and work with youth will find this book to be a valuable new resource. It deserves a place on our forefront shelf.

Dr. Jay Kesler
President, Taylor University

Contents

Before you read this book . . .
A Short Pre-test

What does the word "esteem" mean?

If 1 is low and 10 high, how would you rate your esteem presently?

How important do you believe self-esteem is?

What criteria do you use to evaluate your self-esteem?

What causes your esteem to rise?

What causes your esteem to be lowered?

When can you remember your esteem being low?

When can you remember your esteem being high?

What are some things that are affected by your self-esteem?

Are you unsure of yourself most of the time?

Given the task to describe yourself, how would you do it?

Would you describe yourself as a failure?

Does your self-worth diminish when you fail?

Does your physical appearance bother you?

What part of your physical appearance bothers you the most?

Are you ashamed of your accomplishments?

Do you compare your accomplishments to others?

Is it difficult for you to state your opinion before you hear the opinion of others?

Does your opinion change to match those around you?

Do you like looking at photographs of yourself? Do you think you take a good picture?

Are you intimidated around the opposite sex?

Do you constantly ask people if they are angry at you?

Do you feel that you waste people's time when you are talking to them?

Do you pay more attention to criticism than to compliments?

Do you wish you were more outgoing?

Are there people you would like to talk to but you just can't get up the nerve?

While you were in school were grades really important to you?

Introduction

For a long time people have been concerning themselves with the idea of the value of man. Philosophers of every culture and generation have pondered the worth of man. Songs have been sung about it. Poems have been written about it. Like Ponce de Leon, the Spanish explorer centuries ago, self-esteem is today's fountain of youth for which people are looking. It was de Leon's belief that if he could find this fountain, he could live longer. People today search for who they are and why they are alive as reasons to live longer. Self-esteem answers both of these questions.

Much has been said about self-esteem and the value of man. Ralph Waldo Emerson said, "What lies behind us and what lies before us are tiny matters compared to what lies within us." John Powell wrote, "Of course, it may be that you or I should change something in our lives, but I think it is much more realistic and important to change something in ourselves. It may be that the parasites which are eating away inside us, depriving us of the deeper joys and satisfactions of life, should become the object of our attention." One of the "parasites" is low self-esteem!

The debate about self-esteem has been going on for years. Almost 30 years ago Dr. Rollo May stated, "The critical battles between approaches to psychology . . . in our culture in the next decades, I propose, will be on the battle ground of the image of man."[1] This is exactly what is happening with psychology and Christianity. They are debating the true nature and value of man.

The topic of self-esteem is very much in vogue in our society today. Most, if not all, of the introductions to Psychology textbooks deal with it to some extent. Many abnormal Psychology textbooks deal with it as well. While at the library at the university where my main office is located, I looked up on the computer the listing of magazine articles written on the topic of self-esteem. The computer said there were 5,976 articles that dealt with the topic.

I narrowed down the topic by looking up the articles that dealt with body image — there were only 232 articles on this topic. The library also had 20 books written on the topic of self-esteem in adolescents. It was not surprising that many of the books I looked for were checked out.

Schools (from elementary to college) are doing workshops and classes that deal with the topic. Corporations to kindergartens are getting on the bandwagon. Many of these seminars address the topic of feeling good about yourself. They are designed to motivate people to be better. They teach people that they are great, wonderful and full of potential. Some of these seminars can be so superficial they only give a false, temporary boost to self-esteem. They put a bandaid on a broken arm. They only delay the eventual fall of the esteem. This book is not designed to do this. It is designed to teach people who they are in the eyes of their creator. It is designed to teach people how valuable they are. It is designed to give people God's perception on self-esteem and not the world's.

This book will not cover **self-esteem** as many books have already done. This book will be addressing "Christ's esteem" for us. This book will show how important it is that a person build his or her esteem from God's side of the cross at Calvary and not their side of the cross. Accepting that Christ died for us willingly (John 10:18) should be the centerpiece of self-esteem. Let's begin this journey of self identity and esteem by looking at what self-esteem is and is not.

Notes

1. Rollo May, *Psychology and the Human Dilemma* (New York: Van Nostrand Reinhold, 1967), p. 90.

1 What Is Self-Esteem? What Is Low Self-Esteem?

They come as Timmies and Tommies; Sallies and Suzies. Freddies and Freidas. Bills and Barbaras. They are all ages and colors. They come in all shapes and sizes. They are gifted, talented, beautiful people but don't know it. They are models and math teachers, actors, flight attendants and athletes. They are students of all grades. They are "homecoming queens" and "wallflowers." They are "jocks" and "jerks." They make good grades as well as poor grades. They are lawyers and doctors. They wear white collars and blue collars. They are found in every profession and career. They are single and married. They come from broken homes. They come from two-parent families. They are the people of the world. They are the people of the world who have low self-esteem. We can relate to them, because we might be just like them.

Low esteem is a universal problem faced by many people in the world. Every culture has dealt with it; some more than others. Every generation has dealt with it. It seems that the next generation has a more severe problem with it than the preceding one.

Life, not a Game Show

When I was growing up in the middle '60s and early '70s there was a television show called *To Tell the Truth*. This was one of my favorite shows. Three contestants would walk onto a TV stage and say they were the same person. Then the announcer would state who this person was and what he or she had accomplished. The whole purpose of the show was to figure out which of the three was the real person and identify the two imposters. A celebrity panel of four people was allowed to ask each of the contestants some questions within a certain time frame. When all four of the panelists had asked their questions they would vote on who they thought the "real" person was. At this point the announcer would say, "Would the real person stand up?" If the imposters got votes they received money for deceiving the panelist and getting incorrect votes. This show really fascinated me. Did all of these people think they were the same individual? Did they all want to be this individual? Did they really know who they were? Was this really just a game show, or was it actual life?

This show was like life — life where people have to figure out who they are and what they want to accomplish. This "show" is for people to figure out their worth. This is not done on a game show where people ask questions. It is done in everyday living. It is the process of establishing identity and self-esteem. This process starts soon after the doctor has slapped your bottom and probably does not end until shortly before burial. At times this process of esteem is like a roller coaster, with many ups and downs.

"Pop" psychology has tossed around the phrases "low self-esteem" and "self-esteem" like a football on a Sunday afternoon in the fall. But what exactly is self-esteem? Even psychologists have a difficult time coming up with a definition on which they all agree. The definition used in this book is: a person's assessment of himself/herself, either positive or negative.

The *American College Dictionary* defines the word "esteem" as "to regard as valuable; regard highly or favorably; to consider as of certain value; to set a value upon." Value can be defined as what someone is willing to pay for something. Self-esteem can then be defined as setting a value upon yourself within society.

Our Value to God

To Christians, self-esteem is gained when they learn how valuable they are to God the shepherd. Paul wrote about our value to God in 1 Corinthians 6:19-20. This passage is vital to esteem's foundation. It reads, "Do you not know that your body is the temple of the Holy Spirit, who is in you, whom you have received from God? You are not your own; you were bought at a price. Therefore honor God with your body." I like this verse because it asks a question. It could be that the church at Corinth did not know how valuable its members were. They might have had low self-esteem as a corporate body of Christ.

Paul writes in verse 20 that we were bought at a price. The price paid was the life of Jesus. He died willingly for mankind. Jesus said, "The reason my Father loves me is that I lay down my life — only to take it up again. No one takes it from me, but I lay it down of my own accord. I have authority to lay it down and authority to take it up again. This command I received from my Father" (John 10:17-18). It was this voluntary death that should be the foundation of self-esteem. This idea will be discussed at greater length in chapter nine.

Since it is through the death of Jesus esteem is learned and given, non-Christians have a much more difficult time trying to figure out their value because they cannot and will not use Calvary as their esteem foundation. Their esteem is based on what is "in" at that time. This is why their esteem is so shaky. They have built the "home" of their esteem on the sand, and the waters of the ocean of society keep eroding it away. They can never build strong enough retaining walls to prevent their homes of esteem from being eventually destroyed by the waves of criticism.

What does the word *esteem* mean as it is used in the Bible? The

Old Testament word can be defined as *to take pleasure in, desirable or precious.* In Daniel 9:23, the Angel Gabriel refers to Daniel as being "highly esteemed." In Daniel 10:11, a man in one of Daniel's visions refers to Daniel as "highly esteemed." Isaiah writes about people not esteeming Christ. Isaiah 53:3 — "He was despised and rejected by men, a man of sorrows, and familiar with suffering. Like one from whom men hid their faces he was despised, and we esteemed him not." The word "esteem" in the Hebrew language used here *(hashab)* is defined as "to think, or account, value or regard." Even though we esteemed him not, he still died for us.

Psychology has come up with two phrases that are closely related to self-esteem. One is "self-concept." Self-concept is a person's perception of his or her personal worth. Another phrase is "self-worth." The few times this phrase is used, it is synonymous with the phrase self-esteem. One of the many problems with psychology, is that even though it uses these terms, it has never been able to establish a unified definition and consistent measure of human, personal worth. In the "hippie era" people would say that they were having an identity crisis. They would often go off to "find themselves." This process might lead them to Colorado and the Rocky Mountains; or to trying to find themselves through hallucinogenic drugs. It might lead them to hours upon hours of analysis. This identity crisis is the same as having low self-esteem, only packaged another way. It is not knowing who you are and what you are worth.

Doctrine of the Devil

Right from the beginning of this book, it is important to write that low self-esteem is a doctrine of the devil; a cleverly disguised and disgusting lie taught by the devil for the purpose of killing, stealing and destroying mankind. Jesus said of Satan in John 10:10, that the thief has three goals, "to kill, steal and destroy."

1 Timothy 4:1 discusses the teaching of the devil and what he is

hoping to accomplish by his teachings. A couple of different versions of the Bible give a clear understanding of his teaching or doctrine. None of these translations describes what Satan teaches, so I will assume he teaches lies about anything and everything.

First Timothy 4:1 reads (from several translations):

"Now the Spirit speaketh expressly, that in the latter times some shall depart from the faith, giving heed to seducing spirits and doctrines of devils" (KJV).

"But the Spirit explicitly says that in later times some will fall away from the faith, paying attention to deceitful spirits and doctrines of demons" (NASB).

"But the (Holy) Spirit distinctly and expressly declares that in latter times some will turn away from the faith, giving attention to deluding and seducing spirits and doctrines that demons teach" (Amplified).

These verses tell us that Satan is hoping people will turn away from the faith and follow his spirits whom he taught. The Bible teaches many other things about Satan as well. John 8:44 says that Satan is a liar, but it never describes what he lies about. It makes sense that he would lie about everything – including self-esteem.

It must be stressed that Satan is the author of *low* self-esteem. I believe that for a Christian to have low self-esteem, he or she is believing the low esteem lies that Satan tells, with the help of society and the media. He constantly bombards young and old with his ideas of who and what they should be. As these people continually change to match the media, Satan continues to develop a more elaborate and extensive stronghold.

The lies that Satan tells must make possible sense. For example, if I asked you to close your eyes and ask me what was in my hand and I told you it was my red Ford Tempo, would you believe me? Probably not. The reason is because the statement is not believable. But what if I told you it was a set of keys, when it was actually a pen. Would you believe me then? You might actually believe this lie. The statement about the set of keys is as much a lie as the red Ford Tempo except it is more possible, and therefore believable.

Satan has been lying to mankind since creation. He still lies today, because it still works. The doctrines that Satan teaches are believable lies. If they were not believable, people would not listen to them or accept them. If the lies were not believable people would not have low self-esteem. The doctrine with which he tempted Eve and Adam sounded believable and good. It caused the downfall and almost destroyed mankind. This was exactly what Satan was hoping.

Satan frequently uses the Bible to create low self-esteem in Christians. One of the reasons for this is due in part to the fact that the word "esteemeth" occurs twice in the King James Version of the Bible. It appears in Romans 14:5, meaning "ordain"; and in Romans 14:14, meaning "to take an inventory of, estimation of." The word "esteem" only occurs three times in the NIV Bible (Esth. 10:3; Prov. 4:8; Isa. 66:2). The word "esteemed" occurs five times in the NIV Bible (Prov. 22:1; Isa. 53:3; Dan. 9:23; 10:11, 19). Since it does not occur frequently in Scripture, Satan teaches that self-esteem is not biblical. He also teaches that low self-esteem should be part of a Christian's lifestyle.

Self-Esteem and Life

As stated previously, a person's self-esteem affects every area of life. There are three major areas that it affects the most.

The first thing affected by a person's low esteem is **Relationships**. People with low esteem are drawn to any relationship where they can get recognition and acceptance. They build their esteem from the relationship. A low self-esteem can have some very destructive effects on relationships. Josh McDowell wrote, "A poor self-image is one of the prime causes of problems in marital intimacy today. If you don't have a healthy self-acceptance, how can you expect your mate to accept you for who you are?"[1]

Self-esteem affects intimacy. Josh McDowell explained, "Even in the Masters and Johnson sex therapy clinics, less than ten percent of the time with clients is spent dealing with the physical aspects of sex. Ninety percent of the time is spent dealing with self-esteem and communication. So often the sources of sexual problems are in those areas and not in the physical aspect itself."[2]

Relationship histories can be a good predictor of a person having low self-esteem. If a person has not dated at all, or very infrequently and when they did date it turned out poorly, this is a good predictor of low esteem. Many people in my office tell me they are worthless because they are not dating. The pressure to date is probably felt by late elementary age children. Going "steady" is a symbol or sign of significance and value in Jr. and Sr. High School.

Low esteem individuals will often build or measure their esteem through relationships. Some people will date low-esteem individuals because they are easy to use. This "easy to use" is more than just sexually. Many people who have low esteem give people gifts hoping this will keep love in the relationship. I have known people with low esteem who have given their dates total wardrobes and even remodeled the date's home (only to be dropped later).

Many of these low esteem dates have a difficult time saying no to any request including sexual advances. Many times the low esteem individual interprets these advances to show that the person they are dating really cares. The truth is their dates only care about themselves. To "prove" how difficult it is for a person with low esteem to say "no" to sex, consider an Emory University study with 1000 "sexually active" teens. When asked on what subject the girls of this study wanted more information, 85% of them checked "How to say no without hurting the other person's feelings." I think the reason they checked this one is because they still want the person to like them even though they said "no" to sex. For low esteem people, sex means "security"; abstinence means "alienation."

Consider this example as it appeared in the *Muncie Press*, Wednesday 4/10/91:

Nashville, Indiana
A Brown County man tried to kill his wife five times through suffocation, electrocution and other methods, authorities said.

21

Eugene J. Boroughs III, 37, was charged Tuesday with five counts of attempted murder, eight counts of battery, three counts of rape, two counts of criminal deviate conduct, three counts of confinement and additional counts of intimidation, theft and forgery.

Boroughs was appointed a public defender in Brown Circuit Court and then was returned to Monroe County Jail in Bloomington, where he's serving time for a probation violation on a previous drunk driving charge.

Brown County prosecutor Ben Hoff said Boroughs tried to suffocate and electrocute his wife in September and December 1990.

Boroughs's wife, who was not identified, also was beaten, kicked, confined and raped over a period of *three years*, including a year *before* she married Buroughs, police said.

It is my belief that this woman had such low self-esteem that she believed she "deserved" what he did to her. It had to be low esteem that prompted her to stay in this abusive relationship. It had to be low esteem that prompted her to marry this man. She had to think that this man was the "best" she could get as a husband. She had to think that no one else would want her. Like this woman, low esteem people are easy to rape because they are good, quiet victims. Many victims like the one mentioned above actually end up marrying their rapist!

If the above story is a picture of low self-esteem, then people who have low esteem often date below themselves. This means that they do not believe they are worthy of dating the "decent" individual, so they "settle" for any relationship, even abusive ones. Low esteem individuals frequently believe, "I've got to be someone I'm not to get the person I want." People in abusive relationships usually end up by getting hurt and used. Then the low esteem individual moves on to the next abusive relationship thinking it's normal.

Low esteem individuals will want to leave these relationships, but do not have the "strength." One of the reasons for this is because when they leave the relationship, they lose their esteem. People with low esteem frequently believe "any relationship is better than no relationship."

Many teen magazines today deal with the issue of low esteem

dating in articles and letters to the editor. Many of these letters are written from teens who tell about a broken relationship, stating things like "I can never hold my head high again in school" or "my life is ruined." After the breakup, many of the ones left lonely will ask a very loaded question, "What's wrong with me?" One problem with this question is the person who asks it internally will also answer it internally, causing them to criticize themselves.

This dating pattern of "what's wrong with me" reminds me of the old TV show "The Munsters." It had five main characters. Four of them were very odd; one was a pretty, blonde, female. When the normal, pretty one (Marilyn) would bring guys home from dates, the minute they met her "weird family," (which she thought was normal), they would run away. She would then frequently ask her relatives what was wrong with her that she could not keep dates around. She did not realize the problem was not her, but her strange family. She should have been asking them, "What is wrong with them (her dates) that they judge me by my family?" There are many "Marilyns" in our society today. They are always asking the question, "What is wrong with me?" It becomes a lifelong obsession for them to find a suitable answer.

Another question these "Marilyns" should ask is, "What is wrong with you for treating me the way you have?" It is very natural to blame yourself for the treatment you receive from others. But this is not emotionally, spiritually or physically healthy. When you blame yourself for their actions, this lowers esteem quickly and frequently, permanently.

The second thing affected by a person's esteem is their **Career**. Self-esteem has a major impact on what you do with your life and how far you advance. If you do not feel good about yourself, this will be reflected in job reviews and raises received. It will also be reflected on your self-evaluation of your job performance. Good self-esteem is vital to your career and success. Denis Waitley, author of *In Seeds of Greatness*, calls self-esteem, "the beginning and first seed to all success. It is the basis for our ability to love others and to try to accomplish a worthy goal without fear."[3]

A third thing affected by your esteem is your **Christianity**. Self-esteem is important to a Christian's growth and maturity. It is very important to have healthy, biblical self-esteem when you deal with Satan and his attacks. It was Jesus' knowledge of the word of God and of who he was that prevented Satan from attacking Jesus' young ministry and destroying the only sacrifice that could permanently remove sin from the resumé of mankind. I have known many Christians who feel that God does not love them. They do not feel important to God. They have a difficult time believing that Jesus died for them. They believe he died for others! Their low esteem becomes part of their theology.

Self-Esteem is Not:

People are usually confused about what good self-esteem is. Let me begin with a quote and then by describing what it is not.
Elizabeth Skoglund wrote:

> Many people confuse the distinctions among pride, humility, and a good self-esteem. The problem is not that self-esteem contradicts the Scriptures but rather that the words pride and humility are not correctly understood in the total light of Scripture. Pride in the biblical sense involves a not-honest estimate of oneself. Real humility is simply an absence of concentration upon oneself. It means that while I like and accept myself I don't need to prove my worth excessively either to myself or to others.[4]

Good self-esteem is not the same as *conceit*! The Greek word for "conceit" or "conceits" (Rom. 12:16 KJV) is *par heautois*, meaning an estimation of yourself; the opinion of yourself that is an overstatement. *Phronimos en heautois* is translated "conceit" in Romans 11:25 meaning "wise in yourselves or opinions." The Bible at times speaks of haughtiness. The definition of haughty is being stuck up. It is having your nose so high in the air, that if it rained you could drown.

Conceit at times can be a cover-up of low self-esteem. Consider the following quote:

Even those who we call conceited have a problem of inferiority. They use this stand-offish pattern of social response in order not to be betrayed into those interpersonal relationships in which they are not confident.[5]

In the New Testament, the word "inferior" comes from Greek *hettaomai* meaning loss, or spiritual defect. It is found in Romans 11:12 and 1 Corinthians 6:7. In the Old Testament, the word "inferior" comes from the Hebrew word *naphal* meaning to fall or cast down. John Powell wrote, "Sometimes we let our fears or our self-inflicted judgments of inferiority shield us from taking the risks and facing the challenges of a full life. We substitute 'I can't' for 'I won't even try.'" To a low esteem individual failure means lower esteem. This is why they won't risk or try.

Bernard Baily made an interesting remark about conceit: "When science discovers the center of the universe a lot of people will be disappointed to find they are not it." Archbishop William Temple said, "There are only two possible centers for life — God and self. If we are not becoming centered on God, we are becoming centered on self; and self-centeredness is the essence of sin. The Jews — and we — may seek for the Light of the World, the Life of life, but so far as we remain self-centered, we will never find it." Making "self" the center of your world is conceit at its purest form. It is one of the most common sins of man. It is probably also one of the most desired sins of man from the devil's point of view. This is a strong statement, but it is very true. People who are stuck on themselves have no need for God — or so they think. They only need themselves. They see God and Christianity as being a crutch for the weak.

Self-love is not the same as self-esteem. Paul writes about self-love to Timothy in 2 Timothy 3:1-4, "But understand this, that in the last days there will come times of stress. For men will be lovers of self, lovers of money, proud, arrogant, abusive, disobedient to their parents, ungrateful, unholy, inhuman, implacable, slanderers, profligates, fierce, haters of good, treacherous, reckless, *swollen with conceit,* lovers of pleasure rather than lovers of God" (RSV). It seems in this passage that Paul is putting a strong negative slant on self-love. I believe that Paul is writing about Narcissism. Narcissism is love and worship of self. It is a love that above all other things loves self.

In a book by C.S. Lewis one of the characters, Screwtape, wrote to Wormwood that God "wants to kill their (man's) animal self-love . . . to restore to them (man) a new kind of self-love."[6] This is part of the transformation that Paul mentions, "Do not conform any longer to the pattern of this world, but be transformed by the renewing of your mind. Then you will be able to test and approve what God's will is — his good, pleasing and perfect will" (Rom. 12:2). Paul mentions this transformation again in Ephesians 4:22-24, "You were taught, with regard to your former way of life, to put off your old self, which is being corrupted by its deceitful desires; to be made new in the attitude of the mind; and to put on the new self, created to be like God in true righteousness and holiness."

Jesus taught that we should love the Lord our God with all of our heart (Matt. 22:34-40). The self-love mentioned above does not allow this. He also taught about self-love (Matt. 22:39, Mark 12:31). Self-love is an Old Testament teaching from Leviticus 19:18 which states, "Do not seek revenge or bear a grudge against one of your people, but love your neighbor as yourself. I am the LORD."

Personality is not the same as self-esteem. The word "personality" comes from the Latin word for "mask." Personality can be a mask or cover-up people wear. Proverbs 21:29 states that people can put up a bold front, or facade. Esteem can also be a mask or facade. One of the masks, or facades of esteem is pride. Karl Menninger, M.D. wrote, "By the same time, by the very virtue of its external uses, a facade can bolster self-esteem."[7]

Pride and *arrogance* are not self-esteem. Pride and arrogance reside in the heart (Jer. 49:16). Pride is from the Hebrew word *gaon* which carries a negative description. The Septuagint translates the word pride with two words: *hubris*, meaning insolence or arrogance, and *huperephania*, meaning arrogance, haughtiness and pride.

Arrogance is like the sin of idolatry (1 Sam. 15:23). The "idol" is the "self." A recent study published in the American Psychological Association journal showed a link between high aggressiveness and unusually high self-esteem. This study reported that there is a real danger in building people's esteem too high. This research study showed that people who are wife-beaters "consistently express favorable views of themselves." This "idolatry" could be what prompts the violence.

Pride is a confusing emotion. First it appears that *pride and arrogance are often indications of too high self-esteem*! Joseph Boden, a University of Virginia postdoctoral research associate commented, "You've got a lot of people running around with seriously inflated egos who come crashing down to earth all the time." Shelby Steele, a Stanford University research fellow, said, "The whole emphasis on culture and self-esteem will never work. It will just add to the grandiosity."

I recently saw a T-shirt bearing the slogan "Pride: It's a self thing." Richard E. Leakey said, "To have arrived on this earth as the product of a biological accident, only to depart through human arrogance, would be the ultimate irony." Man's creation was not a biological accident, but man can definitely depart this life in human arrogance. Pride, described as too high an opinion of the self, caused Lucifer (Isa. 14:11-15), King Herod (Acts 12:21-25), King David (2 Sam. 11:1-5), and King Saul (1 Sam. 13:1-14; 15:1-9, 17-21) trouble and led to their eventual destruction and downfall. It caused the country of Israel to lose battles because they refused to listen to what God said. In Deuteronomy 1:41-46 God told Israel not to attack their enemy because God would not be with them and they would be defeated. Israel attacked them anyway and lost!

Secondly *pride and arrogance are often a cover for low self-esteem*. A person in this category uses pride and arrogance to cover up and compensate for having a low self-esteem. These people are like puffer fish. They try to impress others to cover up their low esteem. These people become shadows of images, hoping to appear bigger than what they actually are.

The effects of pride and arrogance are many. There are some arrogant people in this world who will only look at others if they act as a mirror. Marshall Lurnsden said, "There is only one thing that can keep growing without nourishment: the human ego." Pride causes people to become their own God and have their own laws (Hab. 1:7, 11). Pride causes people to stop praying. Pride causes a fall. Proverbs 18:12 — "Before his downfall a man's heart is proud, but humility comes before honor."

The Bible speaks a lot about pride and arrogance (usually it teaches against it):

Proverbs 8:13 — Wisdom hates pride and it is linked with arrogance in this verse.

Proverbs 16:18 — Pride goes before destruction. It is linked with a haughty spirit.

Proverbs 21:4 — Pride is from the heart and it is sin! It is again linked with haughtiness.

Proverbs 26:12 — Pride can be described as being wise in your own eyes. There is more hope for a fool than for a prideful man.

Proverbs 27:2 — Pride is a form of self-praise and adoration. Wilson Mizner said, "Don't talk about yourself; it will be done when you leave."

Proverbs 28:25-26 — Pride can be described as trusting in yourself. Jeremiah 17:5-8 says that when a man trusts in himself, he is under a curse.

Isaiah 5:21 — Pride can be described as being wise and clever in your own eyes. Jeremiah 9:23-25 states, "This is what the LORD says: 'Let not the wise man boast of his wisdom or the strong man boast of his strength or the rich man boast of his riches, but let him who boasts boast about this: that he understands and knows me, that I am the LORD, who exercises kindness, justice and righteousness on the earth, for in these I delight.'"

Psalm 119:21 — God rebukes the arrogant. They are under a *curse*, and they stray from God's commands.

2 Corinthians 10:17-18 — If people boast, they should boast about the Lord and not themselves. The man who boasts about himself (commends himself) is not approved by God.

False self-esteem can be gained through loving and doing sinful behaviors. Psalm 66:18 states that people can cherish sin. Sin is frequently glorified in the media. People who have done sinful things are prideful and frequently held in honor and esteemed by society. The book of Isaiah predicts an end to this kind of behavior. Isaiah 32:5 — "No longer will the fool be called noble nor the scoundrel be highly respected."

Look at all the examples of sinful behaviors on daytime talk shows. There are now approximately 20 talk shows. New talk shows seem to be springing up daily. Many of these programs glorify sexually immoral behaviors and lifestyles. People appear on these shows and in prideful arrogance brag about their sinful behaviors. Some of these shows' themes are "My husband and his paramour," "My husband does not know I'm homosexual," "Gays and their lovers," and "My sister does not approve of me being a stripper." This is not family programming. Neither is it good esteem-building programming.

Building esteem on sinful behaviors is very unhealthy. Hugh Grant, a Hollywood actor from Britain, was recently arrested in Hollywood for the solicitation of a prostitute. On Monday July 10, 1995 he appeared on *The Tonight Show With Jay Leno*. The audience applauded him at great length when he came on the set. Does this verify that our society praises and builds its esteem on sin? I think so.

One of my favorite shows on television is on the Entertainment Network. It is called *Talk Soup*. This show gives a brief summary of some of the talk shows of the previous week from a comedy point of view. It amazes me that people would want to be in front of the nation and brag about their behaviors.

Low Self-Esteem Is:

Low self-esteem is a series of ambivalent feelings toward the self. Ambivalent means both negative and positive. These feelings usually depend on what is happening that day. It is almost like a person is having a bad "self" day instead of a bad hair day.

Low self-esteem is actually a form of self-hate, self-disgust, self-resentment, self-abuse, self-abasement, self-neglect and is very self-defeating. Low self-esteem is the denial of the God given value and worth of man.

There are several different types of low self-esteem mentioned in *Taber's Cyclopedia Medical Dictionary.*[8]

Self-Esteem, Chronic Low

Definition: longstanding negative self-evaluation or feelings about self or self-capabilities.

Symptoms: Hesitant to try new things, frequent lack of success in work or other life events. Overly conforming, dependent on other's opinions, lack of eye contact, non-assertive, passive, indecisive, excessively seeks reassurance.

Self-Esteem, Disturbed

Definition: negative self-evaluation or feelings about self or self-capabilities which may be directly or indirectly expressed.

Symptoms: Hesitant to try new things/situations, hypersensitive to slight or criticism, grandiosity, denial of problems obvious to others, projection of blame/responsibility for problems, rationalizing personal failures.

Self-Esteem, Situational low

Definition: negative self-evaluation or feelings about self which develop in response to a loss or change in an individual who previously had a positive self-evaluation.

Symptom: Difficulty making decisions.

Self-Esteem Is:

Self-esteem is your internal self-portrait. It is your mental picture of who you think you are as seen through the eyes of others. It has many forces that impact it. Self-esteem is extremely important to every aspect of life.

Because esteem often comes from the eyes of others, the word *reputation* can be described as "public esteem." According to Scripture, a person's reputation has some good aspects to it.

Proverbs 22:1 — "A good name is more desirable than great riches; to be esteemed is better than silver or gold."

Ecclesiastes 7:1 — "A good name is better than fine perfume, and the day of death better than the day of birth."

Daniel 6:4 — "At this, the administrators and the satraps tried to find grounds for charges against Daniel in his conduct of government affairs, but they were unable to do so. They could find no corruption in him, because he was trustworthy and neither corrupt nor negligent."

Acts 16:2 — speaking of Timothy says, "The brothers at Lystra and Iconium spoke well of him."

Reputation has some dangers associated with it according to Scripture as well.

Luke 6:26 — "Woe to you when all men speak well of you, for that is how their fathers treated the false prophets."

James 4:4 — "You adulterous people, don't you know that friendship with the world is hatred toward God? Anyone who chooses to be a friend of the world becomes an enemy of God."

Self-esteem is a learning process. It is something that should be continually growing and changing. This process will include learning who you are, learning your value to God and learning about God. The more a person learns about God, the more he learns about himself.

J.A. Hadfield in *Psychology and Morals* wrote:

To see ourselves as we really are is an event of profound importance. It is something brought about by the presentation of a new

31

ideal with which we compare ourselves, as in religion. It can also be brought about by analysis. The purpose of all analysis is to discover the whole person, and to reveal a man to himself. This is always a surprise; it is often a shock.[9]

Accurate biblical self-esteem is built on learning and believing three important things: *who you are, whose you are, and what you are worth to God.* Let's turn now to the four things on which people tend to build their esteem. Chapter two will help us to understand the faulty foundations on which most people's esteem is built.

Notes

1. Josh McDowell, *His Image . . . My Image* (San Bernardino, CA: Here's Life Publishers, Inc., 1984), p. 44.

2. Ibid.

3. Denis Waitley, *Seeds of Greatness* (Old Tappan, NJ: Revell, 1983), p. 47.

4. Elizabeth Skoglund, *The Whole Christian* (New York: Harper and Row, 1976).

5. George H. Muedeking, *Emotional Problems and the Bible* (Philadelphia: Muhlenberg Press, 1956), p. 126.

6. C.S. Lewis, *Screwtape Letters* (New York: MacMillian), p. 74.

7. Karl Menninger, *The Vital Balance* (New York: Viking Press, 1963), p. 253.

8. Clayton L. Thomas, Editor, *Taber's Cyclopedic Medical Dictionary* (Philadelphia: F.A. Davis Company, 1993) pp. 2574-2575.

9. J.A. Hadfield, *Psychology and Morals* (New York: R.N. McBride and Co., 1936), pp. 234-245.

2 On What Do We Build Our Esteem?

How do we "get" our self-esteem? Aaron Wildavsky answered, "Self-esteem cannot be sought as an end in itself but must come as a by-product of meeting standards of excellence — taking pride in work, supporting a family, bringing up decent children, learning about life and imparting that wisdom." Is this statement correct? Should it be?

The above statement is what people tend to build their esteem on, but it is very unhealthy to do so. The reason this is unhealthy is that if you lose your job, or your children are not decent, then you would have no self-esteem. It is also fallacious because some form of esteem is well-established long before you have a job, a family, children, etc. This statement by Aaron Wildavsky could easily be one of the lies that Satan tells about esteem!

Dr. James Gill in "Indispensable Self-Esteem"[1] lists four major scales on which people base their self-esteem. These four are: *significance, competence, virtue* and *power*. Bob George wrote, "People will determine their identities through their appearance, occupation, abilities, family relationships, friends, denominational affiliation, and many other ways. The common denominator of all these human attempts to discover identity is that they are all temporal – they can change with the wind."[2] It is my belief that there appears to be four other major ingredients on which people build their esteem. These four things are:

How People Treat Us

Jesus predicted in Matthew 10:22, "All men will hate you because of me, but he who stands firm to the end will be saved." People who hate us have a tremendous impact and influence on our esteem. People who are good to us have an impact on our esteem as well. The sad thing is we pay more attention to the people that are bad to us than good to us.

Treatment by parents has a big impact on self-esteem and identity. Self-esteem and respect are gained from the interaction with the opposite sex parent. S. Coopersmith in 1967 wrote a book entitled *The Antecedents of Self-Esteem*.[3] He did research on esteem of elementary school age boys and their relationship with their mothers. He found that boys with high self-esteem correlated to mothers or parents who:

☆ expressed affection
☆ showed concern for the child's problems
☆ had harmony in the home
☆ participated in joint family events
☆ gave help that was competent when needed
☆ set clear and fair family rules
☆ were consistent with keeping the rules
☆ allowed the children freedom that was age appropriate

It is no wonder then that children from single parent families frequently have esteem problems.

One good parent who imparted high esteem was Mordecai. It was Mordecai who had a tremendous impact on Queen Esther's esteem. Mordecai was Esther's cousin. When her parents died, he took her in as his own daughter (Esth. 2:7). In this verse, Esther is described as being "lovely in form and features." One of the things

Mordecai taught her was to be humble. Esther 2:15 describes her, "When the turn came for Esther (the girl Mordecai had adopted, the daughter of his uncle Abihail) to go to the king, she asked for nothing other than what Hegai, the king's eunuch who was in charge of the harem, suggested. And Esther won the favor of everyone who saw her."

Esther was beautiful, but humble. What a rare combination. She could have asked for anything from the King she wanted. She chose to submit to Hegai's suggestion. She was obedient to others and this made her beautiful. According to 1 Peter 3:5-6, it was this submissive spirit that made the "holy women of the past who put their hope in God used to make themselves beautiful. They were submissive to their own husbands, like Sarah, who obeyed Abraham and called him her master. You are her daughters if you do what is right and do not give way to fear."

Children get their models of what they should be like from the same sex parent. Josh McDowell wrote, "A boy with an ineffective father relationship grows up with a poor sense of masculinity. He has little confidence in himself as a male human being. Since he lacked an effective relationship with his dad, it is difficult for him to know how to 'be a man.'"[4] The role model is the same sex parent. What you see from this parent you consider normal. You become what they became (Ezek. 16:44). This is why being and having a good role model is so important.

Many questions are asked about parenting. Ruth Stafford Peale was asked the question, "Can parents really do much to encourage self-reliance?" She responded, "Yes, they can." She continued:

> The secret is this: watch to see where a child's innate skills and talents lie, then gently (do not expect too much too soon) lead or coax him or her in those areas. It may be difficult for a father who was a crack athlete to understand and help a son who would rather play chess than football. But chess, not football, is what such a boy needs if confidence is to grow up in him. If he does that one thing well he will come to believe that he can do other things well, and he won't be afraid to attempt them.[5]

This is one of the reasons I like "Promise Keepers." They strive for: ethical integrity, seeking God's will, strengthened marriages, unity of all Christians, racial reconciliation, love and discipline for their children, sexual purity, allowing God to use them to touch their world, and honoring God above all else. What a great role model these people could be if they honored all of these "promises."

A tale of three biblical characters will show the impact of either choosing to put your esteem in people's treatment of you, or choosing not to. The men are Haman, Nehemiah and Zacchaeus.

In the book of Esther there is a man named Haman who built his esteem on how people treated him. He actually built his esteem on whether people bowed to him or feared him. In Esther 5:9 it records, "Haman went out that day happy and in high spirits. But when he saw Mordecai at the king's gate and observed that he neither rose nor showed fear in his presence, he was filled with rage against Mordecai." Mordecai's lack of "respect" to Haman must have affected Haman's self-esteem. In Esther 10:3 it reveals that Mordecai was "preeminent among the Jews, and held in high esteem by his many fellow Jews, because he worked for the good of his people and spoke up for the welfare of all the Jews." This really had to anger Haman. It was partly his low esteem that hung him!

Nehemiah is a person who put his esteem in what God told him to accomplish; not in how men treated him. If he had built his esteem on how people treated him, the wall would never have been built. Nehemiah 2:10 states that Sanballat and Tobiah were disturbed because Nehemiah "had come to promote the welfare of the Israelites." In Nehemiah 2:19 Sanballat, Tobiah, and Geshem mocked and ridiculed Nehemiah and the people rebuilding the wall. Nehemiah completed this task because he did not put his esteem in people's treatment of him.

Luke 19 tells about Zacchaeus who could have been the easiest person to have his esteem lowered by people's opinion of him. He was an easy target because of at least three reasons: 1) he worked for the Roman government as a tax collector and was hated by the Jews, 2) he was very rich, and 3) he was very short. Jesus met him when he was up in a tree. What Jesus did with him had to shock not only Zacchaeus but the other Jews as well. Jesus told him, "Zacchaeus, come down immediately. I must stay at your house today" (Luke 19:5). Jesus possibly improved Zacchaeus' self-esteem by his mere presence and how he treated him! It would be great if all people who become Christians would gain esteem from their relationship to Christ.

People's Verbal Opinion of Us

Jesus warned in Luke 6:26, "Woe to you when all men speak well of you, because this is how your fathers treated the false prophets." Many people who have low esteem want everyone to like and speak well of them.

The problem with this is that people don't know everyone, so everyone cannot like them. Paul wrote about this issue in Galatians 1:10, "Am I now trying to win the approval of men, or of God? Or am I trying to please men? If I were still trying to please men, I would not be a servant of Christ." Paul must have attempted to do this because he used the word *still* in this passage.

When esteem is gained by people's opinion of us, this is "affirmation," or "appreciation" esteem. People everywhere need to be affirmed and appreciated by others, but this is not something that should be used to build self-esteem. David at times seems to put his esteem in others' opinion of himself. In Psalm 22:6-7 David is scorned by people and he feels that he is a worm. This is one of the dangers of building your esteem on people's opinion of you: you may think you are a worm.

One of the "benefits" of building esteem from other people's opinion is that it can give a quick fix to a broken esteem. But there are also some disadvantages. Jim Tally and Bobbie Reed write, "Basing your self-image on the opinion of others is attractive because it offers you the approval and affirmation of those who think well of you. But it also makes criticism a very difficult thing to handle, since criticism is viewed as an attack on one's self-worth."[6]

An acrostic definition of criticism is:

Crushing
Remarks
Involving
Tongues
Instilling
Constant
Insecurity
Suffocating
Me

Criticism is often very crushing to the personality and self-esteem. It is also part of our human nature to be critical of others. People praising others goes against our human nature. But praise from others is very important. Leo Buscaglia wrote, "Somebody has got to come up occasionally and pat us on the shoulder and say, 'Wow! That's good. I really like that.' It would be a miracle if we could let people know what was right rather than always pointing out what is wrong."

Jesus continually had to deal with the criticism of people he was around. His own family thought that he was out of his mind (Mark 3:21). It records in Matthew 13:53-58,

> When Jesus had finished these parables, he moved on from there. Coming to his hometown, he began teaching the people in their synagogue, and they were amazed. "Where did this man get this wisdom and these miraculous powers?" they asked. "Isn't this the carpenter's son? Isn't his mother's name Mary, and aren't his brothers James, Joseph, Simon and Judas? Aren't all his sisters with us? Where then did this man get all these things?" And they took offense at him. But Jesus said to them, "Only in his hometown and in his own house is a prophet without honor." And he did not do many miracles there because of their lack of faith.

Jesus states that a prophet is without honor in his hometown two more times (John 4:44; Luke 4:24). He is referring to himself not getting respect from his hometown folks. It is the same today: we can leave home and get lots of respect, but at our hometown there is almost no respect. Satan will use this to lower a person's self-esteem!

Consider David's esteem again. In 2 Samuel 16:5-14 he was being cursed and criticized by a man named Shimei. He pelted David and David's men with rocks. But this time it did not lower David's esteem. One of David's men, Abishai, wanted to cut off Shimei's head. David says to Abishai, "Leave him alone; let him curse, for the LORD has told him to" (2 Sam. 16:11). David hopes in 16:12, "It may be that the LORD will see my distress and repay me with good for the cursing I am receiving today." Most people respond to criticism like Abishai; they want to counterattack. We should actually be more like David.

Consider the following example about how one person dealt with criticism:

Yanks' Tartabull asks for a trade

For weeks Danny Tartabull refused to respond to criticism from George Steinbrenner, but it's clear now that he took it to heart. Saying Friday that Steinbrenner hit him "below the belt" by questioning his work ethic, Tartabull admitted he has asked the Yankees to trade him.

"It's not like I'm gasping for air where I need out," said Tartabull, who was available but did not play Friday night as the Yanks lost to Seattle, 11-1. "I like this team and my teammates. But I'm upset with some of the things that have been said. If they're so disappointed in me, I would not mind moving on."

It's common knowledge that the Yankees have been trying to trade Tartabull for the last couple of years, only to find teams unwilling to take on his contract.[7]

When I recently talked to a group of nurses from Indiana on success and self-esteem, I asked them to evaluate me. This is risky if you build your esteem on people's opinions. The results showed that 97% of the 300 plus nurses rated the seminar as excellent; 3% rated it good or average. It is ironic, but many people who have low self-esteem would be concerned about the 3% negative and forget the 97% positive. To prove my point, I believe that 49 compliments can be negated by 1 criticism. This is awful, but true. With some people who have low self-esteem it does not matter how many compliments they receive; one negative will delete all of the positives.

People with low self-esteem abhor criticism. Criticism from friends is like being killed by "friendly fire." Franklin Jones said, "Seeing ourselves as others see us would probably confirm our worst suspicions about them." Eleanor Roosevelt said, "No one can make you feel inferior without your consent."[8] James H. Boren said, "It is hard to look up to a leader who keeps his ear to the ground."

Even Hollywood is critical of its own when it comes to body size, shape and tone. *People* magazine did a cover story about body image and self-esteem called "Mission Impossible." The story told about Alicia Silverstone who will appear in the next Batman movie. At the Academy Awards last March she appeared in public having gained 5 or 10 pounds. Tabloids went nuts with lines like "Batman and Fatgirl" and "Look out Batman! Here Comes Buttgirl."[9]

Criticism affects all people, but in different ways. Mary Ellin Barrett wrote,

> No matter how self-assured many of us feel, at any given moment someone's mildly offensive or irritating comments can rock our emotional stability. "These comments trigger in us some intensive negative emotional experience," says Judith Sills, Ph.D., psychologist and author of *Excess Baggage* (Penguin). "They push our buttons, deflating our self-esteem or sabotaging our ability to cope."[10]

Self-criticism is more dangerous to a person's esteem than criticism from others. Man is the only animal that criticizes itself. No cow has ever stood in the field and said to itself, "I'm fat." No ape or baboon has ever said to itself while swinging in a tree eating bananas, "I'm ugly and useless."

Self-criticism is obvious and often occurs when people are asked to describe themselves. It is sad that when describing themselves most people use the *past* and *negatives* to do it! This is because it is more comfortable to be negative with yourself than positive.

Positive statements said about oneself are seen as arrogant, while negative statements about oneself are seen as humble. This is a lie taught by Satan! How can people get rid of all the negatives they think about themselves? It has to come from a new mind and attitude about themselves (Rom. 12:2; Eph. 4:20-24). It comes when God gives us a new heart (Ezek. 36:26).

It is one thing to compliment yourself, but it is entirely different to receive a compliment from someone else. Most people need to learn to stop blowing compliments off. (Which is actually a gentle form of self-criticism). I saw a sweatshirt in a catalog that was very imaginative. It said on it in big, bold letters **Now Accepting Compliments**. I believe that it is important for people to realize that when they receive compliments well, they are actually praising God.

The Bible does not speak much about compliments. It does teach that compliments can be wasted (Prov. 23:8). Compliments tend to test people (Prov. 27:21). Some people are afraid to say "Thank you" when they receive a compliment because they don't want to be seen as conceited. The "test" of a compliment is, "Will you accept it gracefully?"

The perception of being conceited and praising yourself can be supported by two verses: Proverbs 25:27 advises, "It is not good to eat too much honey, nor is it honorable to seek one's own honor." Proverbs 27:2 cautions, "Let another praise you, and not your own mouth; someone else, and not your own lips."

People may see compliments as:

❖ Motivated remarks from people who want something. Compliments are a form of "set up" by the person giving them.
❖ Nice people telling lies.
❖ Deceived people making statements they think are true.
❖ Statements made by people who **have** to be positive with you. These people would be parents, grandparents, brothers, sisters, aunts, uncles, friends, coaches, teachers, ministers and spouses.

Mark Twain quipped, "I can live for two months on one good compliment." This is true only if you believe what the people are proclaiming. This means that he learned to accept compliments from people. People with low self-esteem will only accept compliments from others if they have made the same complimentary statement to themselves. The opposite of what Mark Twain said might be more true, that people can live most of their lives dwelling on one criticism.

People can be either self-effacing of compliments or self-depreciating of compliments. To efface means to wipe out, destroy, do away with. Depreciation means to reduce the value of. People tend to negate compliments and dwell on criticism.

At times praise can be very deceiving. Jesus said, "I do not accept praise from men" (John 5:41). This does not mean that Jesus accepted criticism from men either. Jesus had to learn how to handle criticism. Most people seem to think that compliments are just flattering remarks. The word "flatter" comes from the Hebrew root *chalaq* meaning "to be smooth, slippery." It is used nine times in the Old Testament. The word is translated faithless, flatter, flatters, smoother, smooths (Prov. 5:3; 26:28; 28:23; Ezek. 12:24; Dan. 11:31, Psa. 12:2-3; 36:2). In the New Testament the word "flattering" or "flatter" is found in Romans 16:18; 1 Thessalonians 2:5, and Jude 1:16. The Greek words used here are *chrestologias*, meaning "smooth, plausible speech"; *logo kolaleias*, meaning "flattering words"; and *thaumazo prosopa*, meaning "to admire the face," or "for one's own advantage."

In most of these verses in both the New and the Old Testament, the words "lips," "mouth" or "speech" are used in connection with the word "flatter." This is how most people see compliments, as a form of flattering. Flattering according to the *American College Dictionary* is defined as, "to seek to please by complimentary speech or attentions; compliment or praise insincerely; to represent too favorably; to play upon the vanity or susceptibilities of."

What does the Bible teach about flattery?

Psalm 12:2-3 – Flattering lips are deceptive.

Proverbs 26:28 – A flattering mouth works ruin.

Proverbs 28:23 – A rebuke has a more favorable end gain than a flattering tongue.

Psalm 36:2 – Flattery can even cause a person to deceive himself.

Daniel 11:32 – A flattering tongue is linked with corruption.

Job 32:21 – Flattery is a way of showing partiality.

In 1 Thessalonians 2:5 Paul affirms that he never used flattery in his ministry. He states that God is his witness of this fact.

Romans 16:18 links flattery with deceiving the heart or mind of the naive, or a person who knows no evil.

In Luke 6:26, Jesus gives this warning, "Woe to you when all men speak well of you, for that is how their fathers treated the false prophets." This verse indicates that if everyone likes you and all have positive things to say about you, you are a false prophet.

King Saul is another classic example of a person who built his esteem on people's opinion of him. In 1 Samuel 18:7-9 it reads, "As they danced, they sang: 'Saul has slain his thousands, and David his tens of thousands.' Saul was very angry; this refrain galled him. 'They have credited David with tens of thousands,' he thought, 'but me with only thousands. What more can he get but the kingdom?' And from that time on Saul kept a jealous eye on David." Saul lost his esteem because of this song sung by the people. This song stated musically the people's opinion of Saul and David. This song was very popular. It was sung even in Gath which was one of the five principle cities of the Philistines (1 Sam. 21:11). This must have lowered Saul's esteem even more. If they had Casey Kasem, he would have played this song on the top 40.

Saul was frequently swayed by peer pressure (which is a sign of low self-esteem). Earlier in Saul's reign he had disobeyed God, and Samuel had taken his kingdom from him. Saul asks Samuel, "I was afraid of the people so I gave in to them. Now I beg you, forgive my sin and come back with me, so that I may worship the LORD" (1 Sam. 15:24-25). This statement proves where Saul put his esteem. He was afraid of the people and their opinion of him. The reason Saul asked Samuel to come back with him was that this would prevent Saul from "losing face" in front of the people of Israel. Saul's reputation was very important to him. Ecclesiastes 7:1a states something Saul would have agreed with, "A good name is better than fine perfume."

The Pharisees and teachers of the law had a wonderful way of lowering people's esteem. I guess they should have read the book *How to Win Friends and Influence People* by Dale Carnegie. The Pharisees and teachers of the law frequently referred to the people that Jesus was around as "tax collectors and sinners" (Matt. 9:11; Mark 2:16; Luke 5:30; 15:2). If the Pharisees were arrogant, they probably said this to the people's face. This had to lower those people's esteem. Maybe this is why they hung around Jesus. Jesus rarely criticized. In fact, the people loved Jesus' teachings and style, "because he taught as one who had authority, and not as their teachers of the law" (Matt. 7:29). Many of Jesus' parables were talking about the chief priests and the Pharisees. This surely greatly delighted the "tax collectors and sinners." The chief priests and Pharisees appear to have hated this. Matthew 21:45-46 — "When the chief priests and Pharisees heard Jesus' parables, they knew he was talking about them. They looked for a way to arrest him, but they were afraid of the crowd because the people held that he was a prophet." Jesus' teaching style was comforting, consoling and caring. The Pharisees' teaching style was critical, condemning and cutting.

People's opinion of us is frequently gained from how we behave. In *Breakaway*, September 1993 (a magazine from Focus on the Family) they asked girls the question, "Why are girls often embarrassed to eat in front of guys?" Three of the girls answered:

Nicole: "They don't want the guy to think they're fat."

Emeline: "They don't want to look like pigs."

Kensy: "They think the guy might make fun of them for eating too much."

People's preconceived opinion can even control eating habits and behaviors as well as esteem.

Comparison of Ourselves to the Media's Image

Paul urged in Romans 12:2, "Do not conform any longer to the pattern of this world . . . ." When you build your esteem on the media's image, you are conforming to the pattern of the world. The average height and weight of a female model is 5'9", 110 pounds. Shelley Michelle, who was a body double for Julia Roberts in *Pretty Woman* and runs an agency called Body Doubles and Parts, says that at least 85% of body doubles have had breast implants.[11]

I recently read that five "Supermodels" — Lucky Vanous (34 years old, 6'2", 190), Kathy Ireland (31 years old, 5'11", size 8), Elle MacPherson (31 years old, 6', 125 lbs.), Rachel Hunter (25 years old, 6', 145 lbs.), and Claudia Schiffer (24 years old, 5'11", size 4-6) have come out with exercise videos. Just for your information the average woman in America is 5'4", 140 lbs and size 14. The average male in America is 5'9", 170 pounds. These models are nowhere near the average. Comparing yourself to these people could result in a good case of depression and guarantee a low self-esteem! These people are all gorgeous in the media's mind. Claudia Schiffer is probably the one I admire the most. It is not because of the way she looks; but it is because of her beliefs and values. Consider the story by the Associated Press entitled "Claudia Schiffer says some things best unseen."

> Cindy Crawford did it, Elle MacPherson did it. Claudia Schiffer says she'll never, ever do it.
> Pose nude, that is.
> "There are some things I just want to keep private," she said in the July issue of Redbook, graced by her fully clothed self on the cover. "Lots of nude pictures are very beautiful. But this is not my thing."
> Why?
> "It has nothing to do with being German and nothing to do with being buttoned up," she says. "It has to do with principles."[12]

One of the problems with comparing yourself to these people or others from Hollywood is that the playing field is not level. The rules change regularly. Many of these actresses and actors have paid physical trainers who help them work out to look great. Many have their own dieticians who help them decide what to eat. And many have their own chefs who do the cooking. If I had my own physical trainer who had put in my house my own workout room with sauna, whirlpool etc., I would look great too. *Hard Copy* on 12/13/95 reported that one of these physical trainers who has designed customized workout areas for the stars charges as much as $500,000 to retain his services. (This includes the workout area.) What a deal, I think I'll take two!

When females compare themselves to other females, (even those that are not models), they frequently believe that the other women are actually Albert Einstein in Pamela Anderson's body. I have known many girls who consider their girlfriends beautiful, but they consider themselves ugly. The debate between these girls goes like this:

Wendy: "Kim, you are absolutely beautiful. I wish I could have the same figure you do. I feel I am ugly because of my thighs and hips."

Kim: "You have got to be kidding. I wish I were as tall and skinny as you. My stomach is always bulging out. I wish I had a washboard tummy like you."

The problem here is they each want to be like the other person and don't like themselves! Satan has to like this. Satan had to teach this.

There is an old saying, "Clothes make the man." Clothing designers and the media have tapped into it. Thanks to the media, designer labels have become a way that people build their esteem. Some designers are: Bill Blass, Oscar de la Renta, Yves Saint Laurent, Ralph Lauren, Calvin Klein, Jordache, Liz Claiborne, Gloria Vanderbilt, Reebok, Nike, LA Gear and No Fear to name a few. The message given from the media is strong and clear; it goes straight to the brain, "To be someone special and valuable, you've got to dress like someone special." Grady Hauser, vice-president for marketing of Teen-Agers Research Unlimited said, "Last year, America's 29.2 million teenagers spent $30 billion of their own money, much of it on clothing."[13] I guess teenagers have learned the media's message well. Looks are everything according to the media. Jesus taught the direct opposite of this in John 7:24, "Stop judging by mere appearances, and make a right judgment."

Deceptive designers have come up with a new way to make people feel better about themselves. It is called "vanity sizing." This is where they keep the size numbers the same, but they make the clothes larger. Not only are the sizes larger in proportion, so are the prices. This new and improved smaller size without any effort has to give a psychological boost to a person's self-esteem. It is a shallow boost, because the person knows their "true" size.

Our Opinion of Ourselves

Our opinion of ourselves is the fourth block of self-esteem. Proverbs 23:7 states, "For as a man thinketh in his heart, so is he. . ." (KJV). We become what we believe about ourselves. Sophia Loren said, "Nothing makes a woman more beautiful than the belief that she is beautiful." Avon understands how important a person's opinion of themselves is to their beauty. Avon has a new slogan that I saw on one of their sacks. It said, "Because Outer Beauty Begins With Inner Healing." I really like and believe this statement.

Your opinion of yourself is often the basis for your self-talk. One of these self-talk statements may be that "I'm ugly." This is a bald-faced lie of the devil. Ecclesiastes 3:11 states that God has made everything beautiful in its time. All people are beautiful. It is easy to see beauty in others, but very difficult to see beauty in ourselves.

Why do people have a difficult time fathoming what God has done and the beauty of his creation when they look at themselves? They are using the mirror of society and the media to measure their beauty. This "reflection" makes all people (even those considered beautiful) to think they are ugly. This "mirror" has a severe image problem. One reason for this is that critical people become part of this mirror.

It is ironic to realize that the image of yourself you see in the mirror is backwards. When you raise your right hand, the mirror image raises its left. It could be the same with your self-assessment. Most people have bathroom mirrors that should be put in the fun-house at the circus. They do not give a true reflection of your image. The mind interprets this image and this is where the image gets disarranged. Will Kommen made an interesting comment about our image in a picture when he said, "If you look like your passport photo, you're too ill to travel." Most low esteem people hate to have their picture taken, because they feel they look awful.

It is interesting to realize that the word "ugly" does not occur in the King James Version of the Bible. Ugly is a word invented, defined and distributed by the devil. Ugly is only found 8 times in Scripture in the New International Version. Seven of those are in one chapter (Gen. 41:3, 4, 19-21, 27). This is the "ugly" dream about seven cows, that Joseph interpreted for Pharaoh.

If you call yourself ugly, you are actually calling yourself a cow and you're dreaming. The truth is no one is ugly. Everyone is endowed with beauty (Eccl. 3:10). We are frequently taught that "beauty is in the eye of the beholder" and "beauty is only skin deep." Actually the truth is that beauty comes from the Lord and he is the one who beholds us. Beauty is a heart trait!

Paul writes about thoughts and self-talk in Philippians 4:8 — that we should think about what is true, noble, right, pure, lovely, and admirable. This would include the way we see ourselves. We should have positive thoughts about ourselves.

If these four things that people build their esteem on are true — how people treat us, what they say about us, how we compare to society's ideals, and our own opinions of ourselves — and all four have equal weight, this means that:

1. 75% of esteem comes from others.
2. 25% of esteem comes from yourself.
3. 0% of esteem comes from God.

God is our creator and the foundation of our esteem should come from him! We tend to build our esteem on the praises of men, but forget to listen to what God says! Bruce Parmenter commented, "Believers who suffer from low self-esteem do so because they give undue weight to appraisals of their self-worth made by culture, from self and others."[14]

One of the biggest problems with building your esteem on these four areas is that they don't have equal weight. Most of our esteem is gained by people's opinion of us and how they treat us. James Dobson said, "At least 90 percent of our self-concept is built from what we think others think about us. I can hardly respect myself, obviously, if the rest of the world seems to believe that I am dumb or ugly or lazy or boring or uncreative or undesirable." The third most powerful influence on a person's esteem is the media.

What is wrong with building your esteem on these four areas?

A. You are making the assumption that people are correct in their assessment of you.

B. Your esteem will never be stable. It will always be based on others. When these "others" change their minds about you, your esteem changes.

C. Good self-esteem becomes equal to acceptance by others. This is dangerous because people tend to accept us only when we agree with them. The fashion industry is based on acceptance by others and conformity. Romans 12:2 urges, "Do not conform any longer to the pattern of this world, but be transformed by the renewing of your mind. Then you will be able to test and approve what God's will is — his good, pleasing and perfect will." People conform so that they will be accepted and approved of by others.

Self-esteem can either be built on what is seen (which is temporary) or on what is unseen (which is eternal). Paul writes about fixing our eyes on what is unseen when he writes in 2 Corinthians 4:18, "So we fix our eyes not on what is seen, but on what is unseen. For what is seen is temporary, but what is unseen is eternal." Dr. Kevin Leman wrote, "As long as you get your self-image from external sources, you will never be your real self, and you will always be at the mercy of what others want to tell you and how others want to treat you."[15]

Now that we know what people build their esteem on, let's look at what people build their esteem in. (Esteem being built *on* means that this is the foundation of a person's esteem. Esteem being built *in* means the inner workings of a person's esteem. There appear to be at least

Two Types of "Worldly" Esteem

Performance or Possession-Based Self-Esteem

People build their esteem in their mental aptitude, abilities and accomplishments (this is done mostly by adults). This is resumé esteem, or vita value. This is evident by the fact that people put a lot of value on people's titles. Montaigne spoke about performance esteem when he said, "The value of life lies not in the length of days, but in the use we make of them; a man may live long yet live very little."

Spencer A. Rathus and Jeffrey S. Nevid wrote, "To be recognized and respected for a job well done contributes to our sense of self-esteem. For some, self-worth may depend on an accumulation of money. For a writer, self-worth may hinge upon acceptance of a poem or an article by a journal. When we fail at work, our self-esteem plummets as rapidly as our bank account."[16] It is not uncommon to hear people say about money, "If you don't have money you're nothing." The truth is that if you are nothing without money, you're nothing with money. People can gain their esteem by their lifestyle. Possessions can be sources of identity within a community. Boats, jet skis, motor homes, luxury cars and expensive homes can all become sources of esteem.

The idea of performance-based esteem makes people "human doings" not human beings. Performance esteem is often sought as a way of gaining status. This is one of the reasons certain people judge success by how many things a person owns. The one with the most toys wins!

This is also one of the reasons people buy fake car phones and antennas as well as fake beepers — to impress people. Many people are hoping for their "15 minutes of fame" and this is what they build their esteem on. When it does not come, or does not come often enough or long enough, this hurts the person's self-image.

Isaiah 28:9-10 is a good passage on performance esteem, "Who is it he is trying to teach? To whom is he explaining his message? To children weaned from their milk, to those just taken from the breast? For it is: Do and do, do and do, rule on rule, rule on rule, a little here, a little there." This verse also stresses the idea that this message of performance esteem is taught. It is probably taught more to guys than to girls.

Samuel Butler talked about performance esteem when he said, "All progress is based upon a universal innate desire on the part of every organism to live beyond its income." One of the reasons a person chooses to live beyond his or her income is to impress others or to "keep up with the Joneses." Performance-based esteem makes failure equal to being unworthy. This is one of the reasons people who have learning disabilities, attention deficient disorder or have problems reading frequently have low esteem. It only takes one failure then to destroy self-esteem. Jesus said in Luke 12:15 about performance esteem, "Watch out! Be on your guard against all kinds of greed; a man's life does not consist in the abundance of his possessions." Lee Segall said, "It's possible to own too much. A man with one watch knows what time it is; a man with two watches is never quite sure."

The problem here is that people can be possessed by their possessions. What happens to esteem when these precious possessions are gone? It is obvious that they will not last forever. Jesus taught in Matthew 6:19-21 about possession obsession, "Do not store up for yourselves treasures on earth, where moth and rust destroy, and where thieves break in and steal. But store up for yourselves treasures in heaven, where moth and rust do not destroy, and where thieves do not break in and steal. For where your treasure is, there your heart will be also." Hebrews addresses the issue of lost possessions in 10:34: "You sympathized with those in prison and joyfully accepted the confiscation of your property, because you knew that you yourselves had better and lasting possessions." Hebrews 11:16 gives the possession that was better and lasting,

"Instead, they were longing for a better country — a heavenly one. . . ." If esteem were in possessions, they would not have joyfully accepted the confiscation of them.

Esteem should be built on the internal, eternal traits of who you are. The sad thing is that many people build their self-esteem on or from sinful behaviors. Look at all the people who appear on daytime programming bragging about their sinful behaviors. The audience tends to applaud these behaviors. Paul writes in Romans 5:6-8 that God's esteem for us does not come by performance: "You see, at just the right time, when we were still powerless, Christ died for the ungodly. Very rarely will anyone die for a righteous man, though for a good man someone might possibly dare to die. But God demonstrates his own love for us in this: While we were still sinners, Christ died for us."

Another problem of performance-based esteem is that people will compare their performances. One of the most intriguing performance comparisons is with game show contestants. I am amazed at how much information people know about things I have never even heard of before. In a comparison of this nature, I feel very stupid. Can Alex Trebeck of *Jeopardy* really be that smart?

The Bible teaches that people compare accomplishments (Judg. 8:2-3; 1 Kgs. 19:3-5). People will even try to buy what God has given others. When they compare accomplishments, people can become jealous and they can want what God has given others (Acts 8:19). People often feel "big" about what they have accomplished by their own power and strength, but it is God who has given them the ability to do it in the first place (Deut. 8:17-18). This idea of comparison will be discussed later.

Relationships or Appearance

Jesus warns about doing this in John 7:24, "Stop judging by mere appearances, and make right judgment." Mere appearance is one of the ways we tend to evaluate a person's value. Jesus makes a comment about "appearance" in Luke 11:44. He judged the Pharisees, "Woe to you, because you are like unmarked graves, which men walk over without knowing it." Is Jesus making a comment about their internal or external appearance or both? It appears that Jesus' comment is about the internal appearance.

Relationship and appearance-based self-esteem makes a person who has no relationship or looks not worthy or valued. (This is done mostly by younger people.) There are a lot of people who feel like "Cousin It." He was on *The Addams Family*, a character who had no physical appearance or personality: he never spoke actual words. He was just a blob of long hair. Society values models and athletes, not "Cousin Its." These are frequently the "role models" that people have. Consider the following quote:

> A person has no identity apart from his relationship to someone or something else. That's why we will latch onto practically anything in our desperate need to discover who we are.[17]

Having the correct appearance is an important issue today. A survey of 90,000 teenagers by the Minnesota Department of Education revealed that the number one fear of 9th grade girls was about their looks. For 9th grade boys their appearance was their third leading fear behind school and having friends. In another study 53% of 5th to 9th graders surveyed said they worry very much or quite a bit about their looks. 48% worried very much or quite a bit about other kids liking them.

E. A. Douvon surveyed 2,000 girls from ages 11-18. 95% mentioned some part of their physical appearance that they would like to have changed. Most common were facial defects and skin problems. Researcher J. Kevin Thompson in another survey of 100 women who were free from any eating disorder found that 95% overestimated their body size. On average they thought they were 25% larger than they actually were. This could mean that approximately 95% of people (especially women) could have low self-esteem! This figure may be a little high, but is not far off.

What does the Bible teach about appearance?

1 Samuel 16:7 — "But the LORD said to Samuel, 'Do not consider his appearance or his height, for I have rejected him. The LORD

does not look at the things man looks at. Man looks at the outward appearance, but the LORD looks at the heart.'"

1 Peter 3:3-4 — "Your beauty should not come from outward adornment, such as braided hair and the wearing of gold jewelry and fine clothes. Instead, it should be that of your inner self, the unfading beauty of a gentle and quiet spirit, which is of great worth in God's sight."

Galatians 2:6 — "As for those who seem to be important — whatever they were makes no difference to me; God does not judge by external appearance — those men added nothing to my message."

John 7:24 — "Stop judging by mere appearances, and make a right judgment."

Romans 7:22 tells about an inner self — "For in my inner being I delight in God's laws. . . ."

According to Gary Smalley, inner beauty is composed of courage, persistence, gratefulness, calmness, gentleness, and genuine love.[18] Smalley defines courage as "the inner commitment to pursue a worthwhile goal without giving up hope."[19] He defines persistence as "continuing to pursue a goal until it is achieved."[20] He defines gratefulness as "a sincere appreciation for the benefits you have gained from others."[21] He defines calmness as "an inner peace that allows you to respond quietly to a stressful situation without fear."[22] He defines gentleness as "showing tender consideration for the feelings of another."[23] He defines unselfish love as "an action directed toward fulfilling another person's needs."[24]

Consider the following quote about appearance and beauty:

Beauty is highly valued in our society. Television commercials and programs, magazine ads and billboards all convey the message that beauty is to be prized. But very few of us compare to the beautiful people we see in these ads and programs, and most of us are ashamed of at least one aspect of our appearance. We spend hundreds of dollars and an inestimable amount of time and worry covering up or altering our skin, eyes, teeth, faces, noses, thighs, and scalps, refusing to believe that God, in His sovereignty and love, gave us the features He wants us to have.[25]

Mary Pipher, author of *Reviving Ophelia*, states, "Research shows that virtually all women are ashamed of their bodies. It used to be adult women, teenage girls, who were ashamed, but now you see the shame down to very young girls — 10, 11 years old. Society's standard of beauty is an image that is literally just short of starvation for most women."[26]

The advertising media loves people for putting so much value in their appearance because people then buy products of all kinds (clothes, shoes, health and beauty aids, fake car phones, etc.) to build their esteem. People buy things that will identify them with success and value. People buy things that will impress others by saying, "Look at what I am!"

Many products have higher esteem associated with them. There has been a recent increase in the number of expensive gym shoes and blue jeans. A couple of years ago I had a teenager tell me that he would not talk to anyone who did not have "designer" clothes on. The ironic thing is that he was talking to me, and I did not have on "designer" clothes.

It is very narrow-minded to place value on clothing rather than the heart. Many of the magazines that teenagers read have heavy advertising from the clothing and shoe industry. This is because "Madison Avenue" knows that this advertising sells not only products but also beliefs. There are even designer T-shirts that people wear. Many kids would not be caught dead wearing generic clothes. Many kids would not even associate with anyone not wearing designer clothes.

Faulty Foundations

Building self-esteem on accomplishments, abilities, appearance, and relationships is dangerous for the following reasons:

1. These things will change with age and time. What you can do today strengthwise, you won't be able to do in 30 years. If you put

your esteem in your strength today, you may not have esteem tomorrow.

2. What society considers pretty and successful today will change tomorrow. If you could go back and look at some magazines 20 or 30 years ago and look at what was considered beautiful, it probably would not be considered beautiful today. Pretty is defined as: delicate, graceful, attractive. This word does not occur in the NIV or KJV. It occurs once in NASB (Jeremiah 46:20) stating that Egypt is a pretty heifer.

3. Basing esteem on physical appearance and accomplishments is superficial and vain. Rick Aberman, a sports psychologist who works with many of the athletic teams at the University of Minnesota said, "Athletes' lives are externalized. Their whole sense of self is based on achievement. Their self-esteem is based on how many people know what they do. That's not necessarily a bad thing, but it leaves them vunerable."[27] If a person builds their self-esteem on achievements, they are vunerable and destined to have low self-esteem.

What happens to athletes who cannot compete and win like they used to? What happens to models who can't model anymore? What happens to stewardesses who don't meet the height and weight requirements anymore? If they put their esteem in the way they look and what they are accomplishing, they become a "human doing" and not a "human being." Remember the definition of beauty as found in 1 Peter 3:3-4; it's what's on the inside that counts!

Two Images of Self

There are two "internal images" that people have about themselves. They are the two parts of the inner self. They are:

1. *Ideal Self* which is composed of what you want to be, desire to be, strive to be, wish to be. This is what one thinks one "should" be or "ought" to be. Dennis and Barbara Rainey call the Ideal Self the *phantom*. They write that, "A phantom is an unattainable mental image or standard by which we measure our performance,

abilities, look, character and life. It is perfect, idyllic. A phantom, by definition, is an illusion, an apparition, or a resemblance of reality. Disguised as the truth, its distortion is exposed only through a careful unhurried, unhindered inspection."[28]

2. *Actual Self* which is composed of what one thinks one really is. This is who a person thinks he or she is with all their "imperfections." This side of your esteem is greatly influenced by the "mood" you are in. Joni Johnston found that 69 percent of women and 42 percent of men said, "their perception of their looks depended on the mood they were in. Thirty-eight percent of the women and 18 percent of the men strongly agree with this body/mood connection."[29]

What happens when these two images don't match up? The bigger the discrepancy between these two images, the lower the esteem will be. This discrepancy might even create self-hatred and eating disorders in order to resolve this conflict. When there is a chasm between the ideal self and the actual self there is going to be a civil war in the mind where Satan is the one waging the war.

There appear to be several levels of self-assessment between the ideal self and the actual self. It is most pronounced when it comes to physical image. This self-assessment is done in a wide variety of areas — hair, facial features, voice quality, complexion, hands, arms, shoulders, back, feet, size of abdomen, buttocks, hips, legs, knees, calves, ankles, height, and weight. J. B. Sallade in 1973 did a study of obese children in grades 3-5. He found that these children had a more negative self-concept than those of average weight.[30]

Most people would prefer to be like *Mr. Potato Head*™ because then they can choose the preferred, perfect physical physique and features they want to have. Alexis Carrel observed, "Man cannot remake himself without suffering. For he is both the marble and the sculptor." This is exactly what the cosmetic industry has done for people. It narrows the gap between Ideal Self and Actual Self by resculpting the body.

Plastic surgery is becoming more common and acceptable in our society today. Caroline Cline, M.D., Ph.D., who is both a plastic surgeon and psychologist in San Francisco said, "There has been so much social change in the last ten years that cosmetic plastic surgery has reached a level of acceptability never thought possible before."[31] This doctor has a great combination of professions. She can work on the body and mind all at the same time. I believe that one of the reasons for the commonness of plastic surgeries is to feel better about our looks. Many of these surgeries are designed to reshape the body and improve esteem.

Gastroplasty (stomach stapling) and liposuction have become common methods of thinning down. While there is nothing wrong with having these surgeries, what I question is a person's reasoning behind having them. I do not recommend them if it is for esteem reasons. I do not believe that in the long run they will make a person feel better about themselves. They do temporarily until once again they become dissatisfied with another area of their physical body. Plastic surgeries are not cheap and are highly profitable for the medical profession. The American Society of Plastic and Reconstructive Surgeons from statistics in 1990 shows:

Procedure	Approximate # a year	Estimated cost*
Breast augmentation	89,400	$ 1,000-2,400
Breast lifts	14,300	$ 1,000-2,890
Breast reduction	40,300	$ 1,500-4,400
Chin augmentation	13,000	$ 300-1,580
Liposuction	109,100	$ 500-1,480
Rhinoplasty	68,300	$ 300-2,590
Tummy tuck	20,200	$ 1,200-3,430

*Doctor fees only; does not include the hospital charges.

Many of these surgeries are performed to make a person feel better about themselves. They want immediate results from the surgeries. Many of these patients want to look years younger. They want to see themselves as beautiful. It would make sense, though, that if I feel ugly or unattractive, I would still feel the same way after surgery. Dissatisfaction with results of the surgery is one of the predicted outcomes.

Having all the fat sucked out of a person would not change attitude. It is this "attitude" that needs to be altered and improved. A nurse told me that liposuction is very painful. Having a poor attitude about self has got to be even more painful. People often see plastic surgery, gastroplasty and liposuction as a way of remaking the body without much effort. These surgeries can become addictive habits. These surgeries can be seen as ways of instant improvement without effort, but considerable expense.

Which of the four areas do you use to build your esteem? Remember that God, and his value for us, should be our primary building block. When it isn't, we can see the effects of a low esteem. Satan enjoys seeing this in our lives.

Notes

1. James Gill, "Indispensable Self-Esteem," *Human Development*, Volume I, No. 3, Fall, 1980.

2. Bob George, *Classic Christianity* (Eugene, OR: Harvest House Publishers, Inc., 1989), p. 83.

3. S. Coopersmith, *The Antecedents of Self-Esteem* (San Francisco: W.H. Freeman, 1967).

4. Josh McDowell, *His Image . . . My Image* (San Bernardino, CA: Here's Life Publishers, Inc., 1984), p. 81.

5. Alan Loy McGinnis, *The Friendship Factor* (Minneapolis: Augsburg Publishing House, 1979), pp. 98-99.

6. Jim Tally and Bobbie Reed, *Too Close Too Soon* (Nashville: Thomas Nelson Publishers 1982), p. 80.

7. *The Muncie Evening Press*, Saturday, June 10, 1995, p. 27.

8. E. Roosevelt, *This Is My Story* (New York: Harper & Brothers, 1937).

9. *People* magazine, June 3, 1996, p. 65.

10. Mary Ellin Barrett, "Don't Be So Sensitive," *McCall's*, April 1995, p. 128.

11. *People* magazine, June 3, 1996, p. 73.

12. *The Muncie Star*, Sunday, July 9, 1995, p. 1.

13. Sara Rimer, "Teen-Agers Ever Seeking New Look," The *New York Times*, October 17, 1985.

14. Bruce Parmenter, *What the Bible Says about Self-Esteem* (Joplin, MO: College Press, 1986), p. 102.

15. Dr. Kevin Leman, *The Pleasers (women who can't say no and the men who control them)* (Old Tappan, NJ: Fleming H. Revell, 1987), p. 101.

16. Spencer A. Rathus and Jeffrey S. Nevid, *Adjustment and Growth: the Challenges of Life* (New York: Holt Rinehart and Winston, 1983), p. 353.

17. Bob George, *Classic Christianity*, p. 83.

18. Gary Smalley, *Hidden Keys of a Loving Lasting Marriage* (Grand Rapids: Zondervan Publishing House, 1984), p. 249.

19. Ibid., p. 218.

20. Ibid., p. 221.

21. Ibid., p. 222.

22. Ibid., p. 227.

23. Ibid., p. 230.

24. Ibid., p. 232.

25. Robert S. McGee, *The Search for Significance* (Houston: Rapha Publishing Co., 1990). p. 110.

26. *People* magazine, June 3, 1996, p. 66.

27. *The Evening Press*, Tuesday, May 7, 1996, p. 12.

28. Dennis and Barbara Rainey, *Building your Mate's Self-Esteem* (San Bernardino, CA: Here's Life Publishers, 1990), p. 34.

29. Joni Johnston, *Learning to Love the Way You Look* (Deerfield Beach, FL: Health Communications, Inc., 1994), p. 184.

30. *Journal of Psychosomatic Research*, 17, pp. 89-96.

31. Denise Foley, Eileen Nechas and the editors of *Prevention* magazine, *Women's Encyclopedia of Health & Emotional Healing* (Emmaus, PA: Rodale Press, 1993), p. 106.

3 Why Satan Likes Low Self-Esteem

There are many reasons Satan likes low self-esteem. The major reason is that low self-esteem becomes a stronghold that he will use to kill, steal and destroy (John 10:10). Paul discusses "strongholds" in 2 Corinthians 10:4. The Greek word for stronghold used here is *ochuroma*. It means "to make firm, fortress." Low self-esteem becomes a fortress from which he can operate. Jesus talked about one of Satan's techniques before he can rob a person. Jesus pointed out that he first has to tie up the person who will be robbed (Matt. 12:29). Being tied up can be one of the consequences of low esteem. The stronghold of low esteem has two elements: 1. the person feels guilty for their wasted potential – guilty for what they are not doing with their life; and 2. the person feels embarrassed for who they are or the way they look. Self-criticism is frequently a sign of #2.

Effects of Low Self-Esteem

Dr. David Seamands, author of the book *Healing for Damaged Emotions*, describes low self-esteem as "Satan's deadliest weapon."

In his book he lists four effects of low self-esteem.[1] (I have para-phrased his four effects.)

1. People won't accomplish what God would like them to. It will destroy their potential (Num. 13:31). Dr. Seamands says it paralyzes potential. Low self-esteem is disabling, debilitating, destructive and defeating.

2. People won't have any goals, dreams or visions about the future and they will eventually perish. Proverbs 29:18 states, "Where there is no vision the people perish. . . " (KJV). Dr. Seamands says low esteem destroys dreams. Dreams are one of the main supports of life. Elizabeth O'Connor wrote in *Search for Silence*, "We are not awake until there stirs in us the possibility of what we can become."[2] Goals are the possibilities of life. I really like what Mary Kay Ash observed about goals, "Aerodynamically the bumble bee shouldn't be able to fly, but the bumble bee doesn't know it so it goes on flying anyway." People with low self-esteem will never be able to fly, because they keep telling themselves they can't. They never take their landing gear off the runway of life. Their pilot is Satan, and he wants them to crash and burn.

3. Dr. Seamands states that low esteem will ruin relationships (1 John 4:18). Low self-esteem actually sabotages relationships, same sex or opposite sex relationships, even healthy ones in two ways. First, low esteem people will push people away from them either by their words or actions. They actually feel "sorry" for the other person in the relationship. They feel that they are the ugly duckling or Cinderella with a dirty face, and the person they are dating is a prince or princess.

For example consider this sabotage to a relationship. Let's say you are dating someone and continually tell the person he/she can find someone better than you. This plants the same idea in the mind of your date, who eventually breaks off the relationship with you. When the breakup occurs, you will say to yourself, "I knew it." The truth is that "You caused it." Lack of self-esteem demolishes relationships as easily as a wrecking ball demolishes a building.

Secondly, the "esteem" or value you have for other people will either enhance or destroy the relationship. Lloyd Ogilvie wrote, "There can be no deep exchange with another person until we have established the value of that person to us."[3] If you don't value the person you are dating, this will create disrespect and dissatisfaction in the relationship.

4. Dr. Seamands writes that low esteem sabotages a person's Christian service. Deuteronomy 1:26 reads, "But you were unwilling to go up; you rebelled against the command of the LORD your God." Part of Christian service is evangelism. Is a good Biblical self-esteem important in evangelism? Yes! It is what gives people the boldness to tell others about Christ. Is a good Biblical self-esteem important to God being able to use us for his purposes? It is vitally important because the odds against you might seem staggering. I do not believe that Joshua, Gideon, David, Moses or Noah could have done what God told them to do without having a very healthy Godly self-esteem!

Low esteem people also tend to think that the way they see themselves is the way other people see them. This too is very dangerous (Num. 13:33). In the story about the promised land being spied out, Israel was approximately eleven days from the promised land and on the brink of a blessing. But because of their lack of faith in God and themselves, they had to wait 40 years for this blessing. Many of them actually wanted to go back to Egypt.

There are three other reasons Satan likes low self-esteem in addition to the four mentioned by Dr. David Seamands.

5. The way we see ourselves is the way we become. Proverbs 23:7 reveals, "For as he thinketh in his heart, so is he" (KJV).

6. Low esteem can be passed on from generation to generation. It can affect three to four generations (Exod. 20:4-6). Self-esteem is learned (Ezek. 16:44). Low esteem becomes an accustomed way of life (Jer. 13:23).

7. It is one of the worst witnesses for being a Christian in the world (Acts 1:8; Isa. 43:10-12). No one has ever won anyone to Christ by hating themselves or putting themselves down.

The World's Body Image

A person's body image is something that Satan is continually working on. In 1985 *Psychology Today* surveyed 30,000 people about their body image. Thomas R. Cash and others made some interesting comparisons from a similar survey taken back in 1972. In 1972, 15% of men and 25% of women were dissatisfied with their overall appearance. In 1985 it was 34% of men and 38% of women. Most of the dissatisfaction was with their weight. 41% of men wanted to weigh less, while 55% of women thought they weighed too much. 20% of total respondents did not like the way they looked facially. 50% of men and 57% of women were not pleased with their mid-torsos. Joni Johnston wrote, "Eighty-five percent of all women and 72 percent of all men are unhappy with at least one aspect of their looks. In my research, men expressed the most dissatisfaction with their abdomens while women blasted their hip/thigh areas. Women also expressed considerably more unhappiness with and concern about their weight."[4]

Alan Loy McGinnis wrote about people being critical of their body image. "Such obsessions with physical failings are very common. Lauren Hutton says her nose is un-even; Linda Ronstadt thinks she 'looks awful in photographs'; Suzanne Somers thinks her legs are too thin; Jayne Kennedy thought she was too tall when she was young; Kristy McNichol thinks her lips are too fat."[5] Our society would consider these people attractive. Since they don't like their appearance, what chance do we have to like our own appearance? Very little.

Many beautiful people consider themselves unattractive in some area of their physical appearance. In the magazine *People Weekly* there was a feature story titled "The 50 Most Beautiful People in the World 1995."[6] Here is what some of the "beautiful people" said about their appearance. Their attitudes about their appearance might amaze you, but don't forget that low self-esteem is universal. Even the 50 most beautiful people in the world have it. This should almost give people who are not so beautiful a sense of justice.

Halle Berry (model and wife of David Justice who plays baseball for the 1995 World Series champion Atlanta Braves): "Onscreen, my face is as big as a Buick." "I have to make my looks last as long as I can. When they're gone, they're gone."[7]

Yasmine Bleeth: "Most people wouldn't turn away from her 5'5", 117 lb. hourglass figure either, but Bleeth would rather be 5'11". She stated, 'Tall, skinny women can get breast implants, and they become perfect,' she says teasingly. 'But women who are small and curvy can't get leg extensions. That isn't fair.'"[8] One of the ironies of this is that Yasmine is one of the stars on *Baywatch*. I wonder if women who get breast augmentations know they have become perfect. Ironically, I bet they don't feel perfect. They probably still feel they are unattractive. The problem with this does not lie with the need to change the physical body, but with the need to change the attitude.

Gloria Steinem: "But it was only the passage of time — and therapy — that allowed her to call a truce with her looks. Throughout the '80s, she clung to her outdated long hair and aviator glasses because, she admits, 'I thought my face was fat.'"[9] It took therapy for her to make a truce with her looks. A truce is a peace treaty that stops a war. She is implying that she had a civil war with her looks and herself. She is like many people. But she is different because her war with her esteem is over. Many people daily face the battle of low esteem. It begins the moment they get up and look in the mirror.

Grant Hill (Co-rookie of the year in the NBA in 1995, basketball player for the Detroit Pistons): "I'm so thin that when I go to the beach, I don't take my shirt off." "I can't imagine women looking at me the same way I look at Janet Jackson."[10] Being embarrassed for one's physical appearance is one of the signs of low self-esteem.

Cara Oculato (a ballerina): "My lips are very full, very Italian. My feet are always taped or bandaged. When I'm at the beach, I bury them in the sand."[11] At times, it is not quite as easy to bury the part of your physical body in the sand. This burial might take the form of shyness or being a "wallflower." When people are embarrassed for the way they look, they attempt to cover up any way possible. Wearing baggy clothes is a good way of doing this. This way people cannot see the way you "actually" look.

Laura Leighton: She hates her crooked teeth. She said, "Sometimes I want to cover my mouth."[12] People who are embarrassed because of their teeth, don't smile and probably hate having their pictures taken. Low esteem people frequently hate the way they look in photographs or in the mirror. They are very reluctant to show people any pictures of themselves.

Amy Brenneman: "Like anybody, I can obsess about beauty." "The trouble with that level is that if you're not careful, you can live there."[13] At times obsession with beauty can lead to eating disorders.

Vanessa Marcil: "I'm not ready to be a woman yet." "I'd like it if my body were more boyish. Maybe I'll like my curves when I'm older, but right now they kind of make me squirm."[14] Don't forget, according to *People Magazine*, she is beautiful.

Realize that these people are considered the most beautiful people in America. If they don't like the way the they look, what does that tell people who did not make the list? They probably don't like the way they look either.

Reasons for Self-Abasement

What prompts a person to become self-abasing? Part of it is because of guilt from sins in the past (Ezra 9:5). But part of it has to do with how man views humility. A lot of people think that humble means to not appreciate or love yourself. Loving your neighbor as yourself is a very biblical idea (Lev. 19:18; Matt. 19:19; 22:39; Mark 12:31; Luke 10:27; Rom. 13:9). Every person is loved by God as well (John 3:16). Francis Schaeffer said, "Man is sinful and wonderful." This is one of the reasons man is self-abasing! Instead of self-abasing, God would like people to be self-respecting (1 Pet. 2:17).

In some people's mind self-abasement is actually a form of worshiping God. Satan has taught this philosophy. This is not true at all. When man puts himself down, he is actually insulting the Creator who made us (Gen. 1:27; 2:7; Isa. 43:7). (The New American Standard Bible in Colossians 2:18, 23 uses the word "abasement." Other translations use the word "humility.") David Seamands wrote, "The truth is that self-belittling is not true Christian humility and runs counter to some very basic teachings of the Christian faith."[15]

If you were given an assignment to write down things you like about yourself and things you dislike, which one would have the larger list? If it is the things you don't like, you're dwelling on the wrong things. You are not following what Paul admonished in Philippians 4:8 — "Finally, brothers, whatever is true, whatever is noble, whatever is right, whatever is pure, whatever is lovely, whatever is admirable — if anything is excellent or praiseworthy — think about such things."

It is sad, but people are taught to always critique their creation. They are taught that there is such a thing as "constructive criticism." I believe that this is one of the many lies that Satan tells. The word "construct" means to build up, while the word "criticize" means to tear down. You don't build something up by tearing it down. It fascinates me that people usually see the flaws in what they have created. I find this true with people who make crafts for a living, or write music. It is hard for people to say that what they made is good.

No Right to Criticize

What right do you have to criticize yourself since: (a) you are created by God and loved deeply by him (John 3:16; 2 Thess. 2:16; Jer. 31:3); and (b) you are highly honored in God's sight (Isa. 43:4; 49:5). The word "honor" here is *kabod* meaning glory, weight, heaviness. Both of these passages teach that God honors us!

Paul asks in Romans 14:4, "Who are you to judge someone else's servant? To his own master he stands or falls. And he will stand, for the Lord is able to make him stand." I believe Paul is teaching that it is wrong to judge anyone, including yourself! It is also wrong to put yourself down.

There were many times Jesus could have put himself down, but he never did. He could have done it when most of the disciples left (John 6:25-71); when the rich young ruler walked away from eternal life (Luke 18:18-34); or when a blind man needed a second touch from Jesus to see clearly (Mark 8:22-26). He never once criticized himself. We should follow his example. Paul commands in Ephesians 5:1-2, "Be imitators of God, therefore, as dearly loved children and live a life of love, just as Christ loved us and gave himself up for us as a fragrant offering and sacrifice to God."

It amazes me that we cannot see the beauty of God's creation that is found in us, God's most precious creation. We live right in the middle of God's creative ability, the world. We are the pinnacle of God's creative ability. All of creation shows how creative and awesome God is. From the honeybee to the blue whale, from the spider to the seal, all creatures great and small glorify God and show his personality.

How can a person look at the Grand Canyon and be amazed; look at the Rocky Mountains and be in awe, but look in the mirror and think that what they see is disgusting? It is because man has not learned that he is at the top of the creation scale and not the bottom. It is a sin to be amazed at God's creation and not see God's glory when one looks into the mirror. I know that this is a very strong statement, but I believe it to be very true.

"How do I look?" is a truly vital question people ask. This is a loaded question. If you tell them they look fine, they probably won't believe you. If you tell them what they believe to be true, they will be mad at you. The person who is asked this question is in a no-win situation. It is best if this person just remain quiet! Josh McDowell talked about this when he said, "What we see in the mirror is interpreted largely by others' opinions about us that we hear and remember."[16] It is important to realize that the image in the mirror is 100 percent backwards all the time. If writing is backwards in the mirror your image is backwards in the mirror. To prove this point, go to a mirror and raise your right hand. The mirror's image raised its left hand. I believe this is one of the reasons people don't like they way they look in the mirror.

Is it true that if people saw you the same way that you see yourself, you would actually hate their guts? If they agreed with your insult, this would make them an enemy. But, if they disagree with your insult of yourself, you think they are lying. Once again, they are in a no-win situation, and so are you. You may never see yourself the same way God does. Isaiah 55:8-9 — "'For my thoughts are not your thoughts, neither are your ways my ways,' declares the LORD. 'As the heavens are higher than the earth, so are my ways higher than your ways and my thoughts than your thoughts.'" Part of this could be due to the belief that what God states about us is too good to be true.

It is irrational to believe that the way we see ourselves is the way we really are! If your opinion of yourself is true, do you think Jesus would have died for you? First Timothy 4:4 — "For everything God created is good, and nothing is to be rejected if it is received with thanksgiving." This verse states that we are at least partly good. Genesis 1:31 — "God saw all that he had made, and it was very good." One of the reasons we have a difficult time understanding that we are partly good is found in 2 Corinthians 4:4 which basically states that the god of this age has blinded the minds of unbelievers. This is one of the major reasons people have low esteem. They have been blinded so they cannot see their true goodness and worth.

We learn in Genesis 1:27 that we were made in the image of God. Psalm 34:8 invites, "Taste and see that the LORD is good; blessed is the man who takes refuge in him." What are some of the ways we are like God? We both have emotions, thoughts, feelings, personality and can create things. We are both good (Jeremiah 33:11; Psalm 106:1; 136:1)! The Hebrew word is *tob* which denotes goodness and desirability. It is also used as the word "beautiful." This will be discussed later in more detail.

I am amazed that people cannot see the beauty in themselves, but I am not surprised by it. I have been around many beautiful people who have absolutely no clue as to how beautiful they are. I wish people were more like David. He wrote in Psalm 139:13-14, "For you created my inmost being; you knit me together in my mother's womb. I praise you because I am fearfully and wonderfully made; your works are wonderful, I know that full well." Verse 13 in the KJV reads, "For thou hast possessed my reins; thou hast covered me in my mother's womb." The Hebrew word for "covered" here is *sakak*, meaning to weave together. God weaved and knitted mankind together with great skill, care and thought.

David knew that God created him wonderfully. Every person who has lived on the earth, or will live on the earth is beautiful because they are all created in God's image (Gen. 1:27; Psa. 27:4). The word "create" – *bara* – means to make (Gen. 2:3; Isa. 40:26; 42:5). The word "form" – *yasar* – technically a potter's term meaning to form, mold or fashion, is used to describe God's creation of us. It is found in Jeremiah 18:4, 6; Genesis 2:7; Isaiah 43:1, 7; 44:2, 24; 45:7; Amos 4:13. In Isaiah 45:18 both words are used. Psalm 27:4 states that the LORD is beautiful. The Hebrew word for "beauty" is *no'am*, meaning delightfulness, pleasantness, loveliness. Let me say it again, because we were made in the LORD's image, and He is beautiful, we have to be beautiful.

David wrote in Psalm 139 that God ordained him for a set purpose before his birth. There are many other people that God ordained before their birth. Some are: Samson (Judg. 13:2-5); Samuel (1 Sam. 1:11-20); Paul (Gal. 1:15); John the Baptist (Luke 1:13-17); Jeremiah (Jer. 1:5) and Josiah (1 Kgs. 13:2).

The Bible says we are beautiful! Isaiah 4:2 claims that the "Branch of the LORD will be beautiful and glorious . . . ." Later, in Isaiah 28:5, "In that day the LORD Almighty will be a glorious crown, a beautiful wreath for the remnant of his people." Since God is beautiful, therefore, we are also beautiful. Zechariah 9:17

describes the redeemed of the LORD as beautiful.

In the Old Testament two Hebrew words, *yapeh* and *tob*, are used to describe the beautiful woman or handsome man. *Yapeh* denotes a trait of beauty that is attributed to the outside appearance. It is used to describe Sarah, Rachel, Abigail and Joseph (Gen. 12:11, 14; 29:17; 1 Sam. 25:3; Gen. 39:6). *Tob* which denotes goodness and desirability is found in Genesis 6:2; 24:16; 26:7; Joshua 7:21; 2 Samuel 11:2; Esther 1:11; 2:2, 3. It is used to describe the "daughters of men," Rebekah, a robe that Achan took from Babylonia, Bathsheba, Queen Vashti, and the women who were part of King Xerxes' beauty contest — Esther was the winner of this contest.

Reasons People Cannot See Their Beauty

One-Dimensional Beauty

The major reason people cannot see their beauty is because they believe in one-dimensional beauty. People get "fixated" on the physical, external part only. It is interesting to realize that external beauty is not of much significance or importance in Scripture. Proverbs 6:25 for example, "Do not lust in your heart after her beauty or let her captivate you with her eyes, for the prostitute reduces you to a loaf of bread, and the adulteress preys upon your very life." Proverbs 11:22 — "Like a gold ring in a pig's snout is a beautiful woman who shows no discretion." Proverbs 31:30 — "Charm is deceptive, and beauty is fleeting; but a woman who fears the LORD is to be praised." Beauty is linked to behavior in Matthew 26:10 and Mark 14:6 when Jesus said, "She has done a beautiful thing to me." Since external beauty is not of much significance to God, I wonder if this is why Satan has people dwell on it? The answer to this question is a definite yes!

There are many people in our world who are "mailboxes." These people are gorgeous on the outside, but there is nothing on the inside of them. Jesus said something just like this in Matthew

71

23:27, "Woe to you, teachers of the law and Pharisees, you hypocrites! You are like whitewashed tombs, which look beautiful on the outside but on the inside are full of dead man's bones and everything unclean." Jesus is saying that image is not everything. In fact, I believe Jesus is saying that external image is nothing; it is what is on the inside that counts. In Luke 11:44 Jesus tells the Pharisees that they are like unmarked graves that men walk over. Paul, in Acts 23:3, refers to certain people as being "whitewashed walls."

Blindness

Another reason people cannot see their "beauty" is because of one of the traits of the Devil. Paul writes in 2 Corinthians 4:4, "The god of this age has blinded the minds of unbelievers, so that they cannot see the light of the gospel of the glory of Christ, who is the image of God." I believe that Satan has blinded the minds of people today so they cannot see the beauty that God has created in them. Another reason people cannot see their beauty is because Satan is constantly telling us how worthless we are, and we believe him. God confronts Adam after he had eaten the fruit and says, "Who told you that you were naked?" (Gen. 3:11).

Stuck Back in Elementary School

Another reason people cannot see their "beauty" is because our physical image of ourselves rarely changes past elementary and Jr. High school. What frequently happens with our esteem is that it becomes *stuck back in elementary school.* Satan absolutely loves this! How did you see yourself back in the fifth grade? Most of us probably thought that we were fat, short, not popular, and not normal compared to the rest of the school. It is not unusual for people to feel this way when they go through puberty. If you go through it early or late you feel weird. If I could do one thing for all 5th through 8th graders, I would make them all mature physically on the same day. This would greatly prevent a lot of embarrassment. Dr. Harry Stack Sullivan "spoke of anxiety as 'that which one experiences when one's self-esteem is threatened.'"[17] Do you see yourself the same way today as you did five years ago? Most people can still remember the nicknames they had in school. They might even see themselves the same way.

Paul writes in 1 Corinthians 13:11, "When I was a child, I talked like a child, I thought like a child, I reasoned like a child. When I became a man, I put childish ways behind me." This would include getting rid of the old image we carry with us learned from childhood. Norman Wright in one of his books wrote, "The image we have of ourselves is built upon clusters of many memories."[18] Many of these memories are of rejection, insult, or abuse. If a person builds their esteem on memories like these, the esteem is going to be programmed very poorly.

In the nineteenth century, William Hazlitt wrote, "A nickname is the hardest stone the devil can throw at a man." Nicknames like: Dumbhead, Dummy, Pigpen, Fatty, Space Case, Airhead, Nerd, Jerk, Dweeb, Weirdo, Geek, Four-Eyes, Carrot Top, Bookworm, and Brain are all common in childhood and can damage a person's self-esteem. In childhood there are four "emotion" experiences that lower esteem. Isaiah 54:4 describes these four emotional attacks as: fear, shame, disgrace and humiliation.

Bruce Parmenter wrote, "Low self-esteem can be caused by a great variety of factors, but prominent among them is loss which damages a positive self-estimate. Such set-backs as loss of youth, prestige, health, a limb, teeth, facial beauty or positive body image due to obesity, can threaten and reduce one's self-worth."[19] If a person had these kinds of set-backs, children in his or her school would have made fun of them. This could not only destroy the person's esteem, but could create bitterness and result in the child bringing a gun to school and killing the kids who are hassling him.

In childhood people may have had their esteem stepped on or experienced "put-downs." (Prov. 27:2; Luke 14:7-11; 18:9-14; 1 Sam. 1:3-7). Put-downs frequently occur when a person attempts to build their esteem by putting other people down. It is making fun of others so you feel better about yourself. This builds a false sense of esteem that won't last long. The truth is, the better we feel about ourselves, the less we are inclined to knock others down.

Josh McDowell wrote, "People with a poor self-image often practice what may be called the double put-down. They either put themselves down, hoping someone else will disagree with them and build them up, or they put down someone else in order to build themselves up."[20] William Arthur Ward made a statement I really like when he said, "The only time to look down on others is when you're helping them up." Benjamin Whichcote said, "None are so empty as those who are full of themselves." Ralph Waldo Emerson said, "A great man is always willing to be little." Our society would be better off if we simply practiced these ideas.

Jealousy

Did you ever recognize that people might be jealous of you and this is why they made fun of you? What are two reasons for jealousy (Gen. 30:1 and 37:11)? What about Joseph and his brothers (Acts 7:9)? People are jealous because of who we are, and also jealous for the relationships we have. What does Proverbs 27:4 teach about jealousy? Anger is cruel, fury is overwhelming, but jealousy is something that will knock us down. When people are jealous of you they may have a wide variety of ways of putting you down. They may make fun of the way you talk, walk, or dress. Why is it difficult to realize that people are envious and jealous of us? It is because we believe that people are better than us, and there is no reason why they should be jealous. The word "jealousy" comes from the Greek verb *zeloo* meaning to seek or desire eagerly (Acts 7:9; 17:5; 1 Cor. 13:4; James 4:2). The word "envy" is from the Greek word *phthonos* meaning a desire aroused to possess something we do not have but another person has. It does not have to be material possessions. It can be relationships, popularity, success, etc. The Bible speaks a lot about envy:

Galatians 5:26 – Paul gives a command for people not to become conceited, provoking or envying each other.

Matthew 27:18; Mark 15:10 — The chief priests and elders wanted Jesus killed because they envied him.

Romans 1:29 — People can be filled with envy. Paul writes that envy is part of wickedness.

Galatians 5:21 — Envy is part of the sinful nature.

Philippians 1:15 — Paul writes that some preach about Christ out of rivalry and envy.

1 Timothy 6:4 — Envy is a result of controversies and arguments.

Titus 3:3 — Envy can be a lifestyle.

1 Peter 2:1 — Envy is one of the five things Peter tells people to get rid of.

James 3:14 — James describes envy as bitter.

James 3:16 — James writes that where envy and selfish ambition are you will also find disorder and every evil practice.

Proverbs 3:31 — We can envy violent men.

Proverbs 14:30 — Envy rots the body.

Proverbs 23:17-18 — Envy comes from the heart.

Proverbs 24:1 — We can envy wicked men.

Ecclesiastes 4:4 — Solomon writes that all labor and achievement spring from a man envying his neighbor. Competition then can be the outcome of jealousy, envy and low self-esteem.

Disabilities and Deformities

Many times children with disabilities and deformities have low self-esteem. The disabilities and deformities may be very obvious. Many people who are in wheelchairs permanently could easily feel unsure, insecure and inferior. Jesus was constantly around people that had disabilities. He met people who were crippled in the legs (Luke 13:10-11). He met people who were crippled in the arms and hands (Mark 3:1-3). He treated them with respect and honor. He refers to the woman who was crippled by Satan for 18 years as "a daughter of Abraham." This would improve her esteem. In some of these encounters Jesus healed on the Sabbath. This proves that Jesus cares more about people than he does the religious laws of men. Jesus took people as people. He taught people they were unique, special and loved. Jesus attempted to restore the priority of people and not the law. This humiliated the religious leaders, but delighted the people (Luke 13:17).

Self-Criticism

One of the saddest things I see in people is that they may be very loving to others, but not very loving to themselves. There is a very interesting question I frequently ask my clients, "Why are you Jesus to others, but not Jesus to yourself?" Part of it is due to the fact that we are more critical of ourselves than others. We forgive others for the same events for which we criticize ourselves. We see lots of good in others, but very little good in us. Shakespeare wrote, "Be to yourself as you would to your friend" (King Henry VIII, I.i). I like what St. Francis De Sales said, "Be patient with everyone, but above all with yourself." If we could follow this motto, we would have a better world.

Receiving Compliments

One of the reasons people receive compliments so poorly is because they do not follow De Sales' advice. How do most people receive compliments? Proverbs 27:21 – "The crucible for silver and the furnace for gold, but man is tested by the praise he receives." Most people when they receive a compliment flunk the test! Proverbs 29:5 – "Whoever flatters his neighbor is spreading a net for his feet." Most people feel very uncomfortable receiving a compliment. Most people become "compliment combative." This means that people become at times very angry when they are complimented. This is probably due to the belief that compliments are not true and the person giving them is just being nice. Compliments are often seen as nice remarks from nice people that are lies. This is also because people become very self-conscious when receiving compliments. There are people who argue with compliments, but agree with criticism.

Self-Consciousness

Being self-conscious is a severe introspection of appearance and how you believe you are coming across to others. In a very general way, females are more self-conscious, embarrassed and humiliated when they receive a compliment about the way they look than males are. Since some females don't believe what the person is saying, they assume that it must be false. Frequently these people drop their eyes or look away when being complimented.

Dropping of the eyes is a sign that someone is better than you, or that you feel inferior. It is a form of worship when you bow to someone because you feel inferior. This is why I like how Psalm 3:3 describes God, "But you are a shield around me, O LORD; you bestow glory on me and lift up my head." I also like what Leviticus 26:13 promises God will do for his people, "I am the LORD your God, who brought you out of Egypt so that you would no longer be slaves to the Egyptians; I broke the bars of your yoke and enabled you to walk with heads held high." Leviticus 26:13 in the King James Version reads, "made you go upright." God wants us to drop our eyes to no one.

Beauty

It is a compliment when someone tells you you're beautiful. The problem is that if you ask most girls if they are pretty, the answer will surprise you. Most girls will tell you "no, I'm not." They might even tell you why they believe they are not pretty. Most girls will refuse to admit that they are pretty because they don't want to be seen as stuck up or conceited. Satan has taught people that receiving a compliment well is the same as being conceited and arrogant. Once again, this is another lie of that slimy, slithering, snake, Satan.

A recent *Hard Copy* did a short segment on pretty actresses who are single and don't have dates. Among them were Cindy Crawford and Julia Roberts. They interviewed several guys and asked them if they would ask these women out. Most of the men said "no" because they thought the women were too pretty and it would be hard to keep them as dates. Most people are intimidated by people that are viewed as pretty, popular and/or talented. This idea is created by Hollywood. The Bible teaches that we should not be intimidated by beauty. Ezekiel 2:6 and 3:9 echo, "nor be dismayed at their looks" (KJV). Beauty then can easily be seen as a curse because of "rejection" from others. The fact is everyone is beautiful and talented (1 Peter 3:3-4; 4:10-11). God made mankind that way!

I frequently ask female clients how they would feel if Pamela Anderson Lee came and sat next to them. Most of the people tell me that they would feel small or ugly. If trees could talk, this is what most of them would feel next to an evergreen in winter. They would feel ugly and empty compared to the beautiful evergreen. They would be leafless and dead looking compared to the evergreen that never loses its leaves and is ever green. I am sure that Satan not only has taught this comparison idea, he also takes advantage of it. He is an opportunistic attacker by nature (Luke 4:13).

Most people receive compliments about as gracefully as a hippopotamus does ballet! Compliments actually are verbal gifts of praise that people give each other. It is important that this gift be received well. A person receiving a compliment must learn to keep his/her eyes on the person complimenting them, not laugh, or roll their eyes. They should say "thank you." When people don't do this, the person complimenting them will see them as stuck up, or arrogant. This assessment is not true, but it is believed.

When people are asked the question: "Are you pretty?" several common responses are heard.

> In my own way.
> I used to be.
> Well, I'm not ugly.

If beauty tends to make people feel inferior, what happens when people hear you insult yourself? Insulting yourself in front of others makes you really "ugly." There is a sequence of five things that take place when others hear you insult yourself.

1. People know what you think of yourself.

2. They are eventually going to have the same opinion.

3. They are going to restate your opinion to you. They will agree verbally with how you see yourself. Your self-criticism has actually invited others to criticize you!

4. When they agree with your opinion and restate it, you are going to be angry and defenseless. Angry because they had no right to say what they said about you. Defenseless because you said it first and all they did was agree with you.

5. They are going to get away from the relationship. Insulting yourself has actually sabotaged the relationship. The word "sabotage" is derived from French workers at the time of the Industrial Revolution who tossed their wooden shoes (*sabots*) into machines to damage them. Sabotage can be defined as "to maliciously interfere or injure," rendering something ineffective to produce what it was intended to produce.

Receiving Gifts

People receive gifts about as well as compliments. Fainting (not literally) is frequently the response to flowers. Frequently heard after receiving a gift is the graceful response, "Oh, you shouldn't have." This statement is a very poor assessment of self-worth. What this is saying is that "I don't believe I am worthy of the gift," or "you spent too much on me." How would you actually feel if the person stopped giving gifts, or he took them back? You would be mad!! But when they give you a gift you are embarrassed. This is a no-win situation, or a stronghold of Satan.

When receiving a gift, it is vitally important to say "thank you." It is a blessing for people to give gifts (Acts 20:35). When you don't receive a gift, you are not allowing them to be blessed. So when you receive a gift from others you are actually doing them a favor!

You are allowing them to show you a sign of appreciation and love. When you don't receive the gift you are stopping them from showing you that they love and care about you. You are preventing them from receiving a blessing.

When you don't accept the gift you are either criticizing the giver, the gift or yourself. Not only does this kind of criticism hurt relationships; it also must be emphasized that when a person criticizes themselves, they are actually doing relationship and spiritual vandalism. They are destroying and defacing something that they did not create and do not own. They are destroying something that does not belong to them (1 Cor. 6:19-20). Self-criticism that destroys relationships is sin.

Some very successful people are self-critical. A recent article about David Letterman reveals, "Letterman is hilarious. Yes, he's self-critical. Yes, he beats the ____ out of himself every single night of the week. He'll sit down with the tape and look at it and complain about his own performance. And to his credit, and to the relief of the staff, he never points someone out and says, 'You're the reason I screwed up.'"[21] Being self-critical has a basis in trying to motivate and improve performance. It does not work. What it produces is a hatred and disgust about who you are and what you are doing.

Satan loves self-criticism because of this outcome. Another reason Satan loves self-criticism is due to the fact that "for as he thinketh in his heart, so is he" (Prov. 23:7 KJV). You become the very thing you criticize. Criticism of others tends to do the same thing. The more people are criticized by a person in authority, the poorer their performance becomes. Criticism of self and others is a disguised, damaging, deceiving, de-motivation of the devil.

Part of our inner healing is the healing of our self-talk! Self-talk is the same thing as self-criticism if the talk is negative. The self-talk of a low esteem person is critical and vicious. It says things like, "I'm a nobody," "I'm too short," "I'm too fat," "I'm not pretty enough," "I'm weird," "I'm stupid" or "I'm a born loser." These are only a few examples of this negative self-talk. This self-talk becomes a prison that can become self-fulfilling. Behavior will correspond with these thoughts. Dr. Kevin Leman wrote, "Psychologists differ on how fast we can talk to ourselves – some say four hundred to six hundred words a minute, others say thirteen hundred words a minute."[22] If we can talk to ourselves so much faster than others can talk to us, what we say to ourselves becomes that much more important.

Self-critical people have a hard time accepting their mistakes, errors and humanness. People frequently criticize themselves for not meeting their expectations. The Devil will pound away at this until the person quits what they are attempting to accomplish. Unmet self-expectations are a common cause of low self-esteem. Bruce Parmenter wrote, "Low self-esteem is universal because no one lives up to his own standards all the time."[23] Thus, one of the causes of low esteem is setting too high of goals for yourself and then calling yourself a failure when they are not accomplished. The truth is you did not fail – because you *could* not accomplish your goal. The goals were beyond your ability. For example, it is beyond most people's ability to bowl a perfect game, but that does not make them a failure. They can still be a good or even great bowler and never have a perfect game.

Self-criticism is not a biblical principle or teaching. Jesus never was self-critical. Isaiah 43:21 teaches that God made man to declare his praise. Insulting yourself is doing the exact opposite of this command. When you insult yourself you are actually cursing God and his creation. You are insulting God when you insult yourself!

Self-criticism may come from internal self-talk statements. These statements are lies that have been taught by Satan. I believe that Moses could have made a majority of these statements to God, when God told him to go back to Egypt and rescue the people of Israel. Noah could also have made the same statements to God about him building the ark. Some of the statements and beliefs are: (The truth is in the parentheses.)

I can't do that. (Philippians 4:13 says you can do all things with Christ who strengthens us.)

I never could do anything right. (Proverbs 21:3 says we can do what is right and just.)

I have the worst luck in the world. (Luck is actually a pagan god. There is no such thing as luck. Success comes from persistence, perspiration and ability.)

I don't have a chance, so why try. (Anytime you attempt something it has a chance to succeed. If you don't try, you have a 100% guarantee of failure!)

I'm all thumbs. (This is a bald-faced lie.)

I'd only get hurt. (There is always a chance for success.)

It would never work. (It is important that you believe in what you are doing. This can be one of the ingredients of success.)

I've never done it before. (Noah never built an ark before.)

It's not who you are, it's who you know. (It is who you are that is a major determination of success.)

I don't feel that I measure up. (God made you special and unique.)

I'm not good enough. (God has made you good enough.)

I can never reach in my career or education what I want.

Paul writes in 2 Corinthians 10:5, "We demolish arguments and every pretension that sets itself up against the knowledge of God, and we take captive every thought to make it obedient to Christ." Would Christ agree with the above "self" statements? It should be our goal that every one of our thoughts be in agreement with Christ. If he would not agree with it, it must be a lie. Every one of our thoughts should be filtered through Christ to make sure it is accurate!

People frequently insult themselves before others do, so others won't. People mistakenly believe that if they insult themselves first, this is good insurance against someone else insulting you. This sounds good in practice, but in actuality this is awful. People more readily believe a negative over a positive. It is easier. It is our nature to be more negative than positive. One negative comment can negate a lot of positive ones.

Questions to Ask Ourselves

There are three questions we must be able to answer to build our esteem. They are:

1. Who am I? (1 Sam. 17:32-37)

2. Whose am I? (Psa. 100:3; 1 Cor. 6:15, 19)

3. Who is with me? (Psa. 46:5, 7, 11; 118:6-7; Isa. 43:2, 5; Zeph. 3:15; Judg. 6:16)

I believe Mother Theresa knows these three questions and answers. Consider what was said about her and what she said about herself. "Mother Theresa of Calcutta had a dream. She told her superiors, 'I have three pennies and a dream from God to build an orphanage.'"

"'Mother Theresa', her superiors chided gently, 'you cannot build an orphanage with three pennies. With three pennies, you can't do anything'."

"'I know,' she said, smiling, 'but with God and three pennies I can do anything!'"[24]

If we like ourselves, what might that be called by the world? We might be called cocky, conceited, proud, boastful, arrogant, egotistical or self-centered. These names that the world calls us are not true. Do we dislike ourselves so we won't be seen this way? Yes. Frequently we feel that if we do our best, people won't like us. So we do less than our best in order to be liked. Satan rejoices in this result.

Let us move away from Satan's reaction to our low esteem. What are the two major reasons for low esteem?

Notes

1. David Seamonds, *Healing for Damaged Emotions* (Wheaton, IL: Victor Books, 1982), p. 49.

2. Elizabeth O'Connor, *Search for Silence* (Waco: Word Books, 1972).

3. Lloyd Ogilvie, *Praying with Power.*

4. Joni Johnston, *Learning to Love the Way You Look* (Deerfield Beach, FL: Health Communications, Inc., 1994), p. 187.

5. Alan Loy McGinnis, *Confidence — How to Succeed at Being Yourself* (Columbus: Augsburg Publishing House, 1987), p. 124.

6. *People Weekly*, May 8, 1995.

7. Ibid., p. 68.

8. Ibid., p. 89.

9. Ibid., p. 93.

10. Ibid., p. 101.

11. Ibid., p. 106.

12. Ibid., p. 125.

13. Ibid., p. 133.

14. Ibid., p. 144.

15. David Seamands, *Healing for Damaged Emotions*, p. 70.

16. Josh McDowell, *His Image . . . My Image* (San Bernardino, CA: Here's Life Publishers, Inc., 1984), p. 50.

17. Ernest E. Bruder, *Ministering to Deeply Troubled People* (Englewood Cliffs, NJ: Prentice-Hall, Inc., 1963), p. 72.

18. H. Norman Wright, *Improving Your Self-Image* (Eugene, OR: Harvest House Publishers, 1983), pp. 7-8.

19. Bruce Parmenter, *What the Bible Says about Self-Esteem* (Joplin, MO: College Press, 1986), p. 93.

20. Josh McDowell, *His Image . . . My Image*, p. 44.

21. "Top 10 reasons why you may not want to write for Letterman," TV section of *The Muncie Evening Press* and *The Muncie Star*, September 3, 1995, p. 1, expletive deleted.

22. Dr. Kevin Leman, *The Pleasers (women who can't say no and the men who control them)* (Old Tappan, NJ: Revell, 1987), p. 106.

23. Bruce Parmenter, *What the Bible Says about Self-Esteem*, p. 145.

24. Robert H. Schuller: *Self Esteem the New Reformation* (Waco: Word, 1982), p. 76.

4 Two Major Reasons People Have Low Self-Esteem

George Gallup, Jr. the pollster said, "If a disease were to afflict the majority of the populace, spreading pain and dysfunction throughout all age groups, we would be frantically searching for reasons and solutions." One of the "diseases" that is afflicting a majority of the populace is low self-esteem. It is my belief that a Christian should never be afflicted with this "disease." Christians should recognize how valuable they are to God. But sadly, Christians are affected with low self-esteem possibly even more than non-Christians. Consider the following poem I wrote:

> A Christian with low self-esteem
> This should not be.
> Why can't I recognize what Christ
> has done for me?

What are the major reasons a person has low esteem? One of the major reasons people have low esteem is that *they value the wrong things* (Luke 16:15)! Jesus said we should first value God and the kingdom of God (Matt. 6:33). He taught in Matthew 10:37, "Anyone who loves his father or mother more than me is not worthy of me; anyone who loves his son or daughter more than me is not worthy of me."

In Luke 14:15-24 Jesus told a parable about a great banquet. There were three things people valued more than God, themselves and going to heaven:

1. possessions (verse 18)
2. work (verse 19)
3. relationships (verse 20).

The second leading cause of low self-esteem is *comparison* (Gal. 6:3-4; 1 Kgs. 19:4). When you compare yourself with someone else, you are actually sinning. Even comparing yourself to a garden hose will cause you to lose. You don't believe me? Can you attach yourself to the side of your house and water the yard? Can we wrap you around a rim and leave you outside all winter and have no damage done to you? Can we put you in the driveway and run the car over you a couple of times and still have you work right?

People frequently compare themselves to "better" themselves. It does not work. The person who compares has to "lose" the comparison or they will be seen as:

1. arrogant
2. conceited
3. stuck on themselves.

Comparison is actually based on feelings of inferiority! This is one of the reasons gym class is awful on a person's self-esteem. Early or late developers get hassled. We compare ourselves when we want to measure up to some standard. It is important to become self-disciplined enough that you stop comparing yourself to others.

Why is puberty so difficult on a girl's self-esteem? There are a couple of reasons for this. First is that all girls do not go through puberty at the same time. If a person goes through puberty early, they might see their bodies as a curse. If the girl goes through puberty late, they feel they are behind and not adequate. Guys have a wonderful way of humiliating and embarrassing girls during this time of their life.

Another reason puberty has some damaging affects on esteem for girls is that when they go through puberty, it is highly visible.

When a guy goes through puberty, his voice cracks and he develops facial hair. Girls on the other hand go through changes that are more noticeable and easy to attack. If I am the devil, puberty is a prime time for me to lower a girl's esteem.

Comparison is done on a wide variety of levels. In *Good House-keeping* there is a section titled *Your Questions Answered by Joyce Brothers, Ph.D.* One person wrote, "My ex-husband recently married a woman who's everything I'm not — she's young, cooks gourmet meals, and has a great job. I don't want my ex back, but I can't stop comparing myself to this woman and reliving everything that went wrong with our marriage. What can I do?"

Dr. Joyce Brothers answers,

> Your ex-husband's remarriage marks the final end of your relationship. You're probably re-experiencing some of the feelings surrounding your breakup. These feelings, as long as they don't go on too long, are part of the natural grieving process, and necessary for putting the marriage behind you.
>
> It's also natural to compare yourself with your ex-husband's new wife. But realize that your 'vision' is distorted right now. When you think about her, you see only the positive, the rosy glow that comes with distance. When your thoughts turn inward, however, you view yourself through a high-powered microscope — one that reveals even the tiniest flaws.
>
> What you need is perspective. Become involved in projects that will stimulate and expand your interests. Get out your social calendar and set up some dinner dates with friends. Keep active and involved, and this storm of unpleasant feeling will eventually subside.[1]

I recently read an interesting statement about Diane Sawyer. The question was posed, "Is it true that the gorgeous Diane Sawyer suffers from a conviction that she's homely?" In reply ". . . Sawyer, anchor of the CBS Morning News and America's Junior Miss 20 years ago, confesses to a life-long insecurity about her looks." She said, "I really have a fundamental belief in the inadequacy of the way I look. It probably goes back to my sister, who was always so lean and elegant and lovely. I always saw the things that bulged, like baby-fat cheeks and a pug nose. Every morning — when I come in for work — represents a triumph over what I've just seen in the mirror." I would like to ask Diane a few questions: "Why are you comparing yourself to your sister?" "What are you hoping to accomplish by this comparison?" "Do you still see yourself today the same way you did back then?" Now that I think about it, these are questions I would like to ask anyone who compares themselves to someone else!

There appear to be at least two common types of comparisons people do.

Appearance

The first common area of comparison is with *Appearance* (Dan. 1:13; Gal. 2:6; 1 Sam. 16:7). This is also one of the things that tends to hurt a person's self-esteem both for males and females. Let me prove for a second that everyone is fat. Suppose you weighed 9 lbs when you were born and you were 24 inches tall. With this same equation, if you are now 5 feet tall you should weigh 22.5 lbs.

Gender Problems

In general three things that tend to hurt a male's esteem are going bald, gaining weight and growing old. In *See You at the Top*, Zig Ziglar says, "My own image improved when I lost thirty-seven pounds."[2] There are several accounts of baldness in Scripture (2 Kgs. 2:23-24; Judg. 16:19; Job 1:20; Ezra 9:3; Acts 21:23-26). In 2 Kings 2:23-24 Elisha is being jeered by some youths because he was bald. It records in verse 24, "He turned around, looked at them and called down a curse on them in the name of the LORD. Then two bears came out of the woods and mauled forty-two of the youths." This tells me that Elisha was a "bit touchy" about losing his hair. He probably could have been a good prospect for the "Hair Club for Men." I bet he wished he could have a bad hair day.

The two things that tend to hurt a female's esteem are weight gain and loss of relationships. I found a sad story about a woman from Cairns, Queensland, Australia named Tanya Graovac. She was fired from her construction job because she was too pretty and distracted her co-workers. She has taken her case to the Human Rights and Equal Opportunities Commission for possible breaches of Australia's Sex Discrimination Act. She later applied for a modeling job but was told she was too short and fat to be a model. I wonder what has happened to her esteem? She was compared by one group of people and told she was too "pretty." Then she was compared by another group, and she was told she was too "ugly." Both of these groups fired her, but for totally opposite reasons.

Influence of Toys

If we could come up with a composite picture of Mr. and Ms. "Perfect Universe" what type of appearance would they have? Their hair and complexion would have to be perfect. Their body would have to be the perfect size and shape. They would look good basically in any kind of clothing. Their teeth would have to be straight and white. Come to think of it, I've seen people that look like this — it's Barbie and Ken from Mattel toys. Does this come as a surprise? It shouldn't. I "blame" this doll for a lot of the problems that teenage girls face today. Barbie is very disproportional in appearance, and when young girls want to look like her, they can take some extreme measures in guaranteeing their success. Barbie's projected measurements if she were a full-sized woman would be 36-18-33.[3] With measurements like this, she might even become a star on *Baywatch*. A recent book I was reading stated that 90 percent of all American girls between the ages of 3 to 11 had one of these dolls.[4]

On the topic of Barbie, there is a woman from London, England named Cindy Jackson. She is 40 years old and has an IQ of 164. She also has had 23 plastic surgeries. Her goal is to look like Barbie. *Hard Copy* on 12/25/95 reported that her surgeries will be finished in the spring of 1996.

Ideal Toy Company came out with its own version of Barbie called "Tammy." She was more proportional in size. I recently gave my daughter one of these dolls. I feel better about her playing with it than Barbie, because she is a better role model. Joni Johnston, Psy.D. also addressed this topic when she wrote, "A significant number of teenagers describe their 'ideal girl' as being 5'7" tall, weighing 110 pounds and having blue eyes and long blonde hair. Many of them also describe her in terms of her resemblance to Barbie."[5]

Barbie is a very poor model for girls to try to emulate. It is my belief that comparing yourself to a toy like this encourages eating disorders and actually lowers a person's self-esteem. Remember that Barbie never has any skin problems, never has gained any weight, looks perfect all the time and is physically "perfect." Joni Johnston wrote, "Girls grow up idealizing Barbie, so they want to look like her. We are encouraged (and taught how) to diet – and we do, even to the point of developing an eating disorder."[6] Most diets have disclaimers that state things like your results may vary. What they are saying is that we can make all the promises about the product we want, but they may not come true in your life. It is usually after doing the dieting that people turn to the eating disorders to lose weight. They now have come out with a "Baywatch Barbie." This TV show also disgusts me. The TV show *Baywatch* would be more appropriately titled "Bouncing Bronze Bodies on the Beach."

Contributions of the Media

Some very popular television shows are also contributory to people having low self-esteem. Some of these shows are: *Baywatch*, (which I have been told is the most popular television show in the world) *Beverly Hills 90210, Hercules, Point Man*, and *Models Inc.*, to name only a few. In 1995 the Miss America pageant was deciding whether to continue to have the swimsuit competition. The television audience decided the issue by a call-in vote. I was hoping people would choose not to have it. When appearance is used as a determining factor it is actually a beauty contest and not a talent competition. In the end, the pageant did have the swimsuit competition after all.

Commercials frequently push body image when they sell their products. Bodies have been used to promote everything from beer to milk and cottage cheese, from autos to vacation resorts. These commercials are not even subtle in their approach. Frequently the cars in these ads have more covering their tops then the models in the car ads do. Why would the media lower your esteem on purpose? Because they know that this is one of the ways they can sell you the products advertised. The advertising media frequently shows a problem, and then it gives their solution.

Effects of Product Advertising

Body image has become a big money maker for the diet, exercise and health spa industry. Some of these people that advertise for these exercise and spa commercials are in perfect shape. They are subtly teaching it is because of this spa, exercise equipment or diet. Heavy people are rarely seen on these commercials. There has been a drastic increase in the amount of "flesh" that appears on television advertising. This is used to entice people to buy their products and "look like we look." Joni Johnston wrote, "At least 50 percent of all dieters are motivated by cosmetic, not health reasons. They are dieting in an attempt to look better rather than to feel better."[7]

The swimsuit industry has jumped on the bandwagon. Many people feel intimidated about going to the beach because of the way they look in their suits. They don't feel they measure up, but that they are the fattest, ugliest people on the beach. This is true for both guys and girls. It is more noticeable with girls because guys tend to cover up their feelings of inadequacy by becoming the "life of the party" or the "class clown."

It amazes me that, as the suits get skimpier, they become more expensive. Bob Greene did an article for the *Muncie Evening Press* entitled *"How tenny-weeny a bikini will American women wear?"* He quoted a United Press International release from Rio de Janeiro that said: "Shapely Brazilian women this season are sporting postage stamp-sized bikinis that leave so little to the imagination that suntan lotion salesmen should jump for joy. Brazilian bikinis have always been tiny, but this year's design — called the 'boomerang' and the 'hang-glider' — are smaller and more outrageous than ever before." Bob continues to quote this release by revealing, "They're so small that 22 of the bikinis can be cut from a single yard of fabric."[8] Can you see why people would feel inferior and fat wearing a swimsuit like this one? Everyone feels like they have to be a "Baywatch Beauty" before they can even think about going to the beach. Both males and females in about equal proportions watch this show, which is even more popular in Europe and elsewhere than here in the USA.

Joan Weinstein of Ultimo said of these new suits, "You have to be extremely thin to wear one of those bikinis — and also a bit of an exhibitionist. They have a different attitude in Rio — we're just not ready for it here. Most American women wouldn't look good with that much skin exposed. It just wouldn't look flattering."[9] Diana McKoy of Bonwit Teller said, "I think American women are more modest than most people give them credit for. If they were to wear something like one of these new Brazilian bikinis, they would be afraid to go outside."[10] If 22 can be made from one square yard of material, that means that the suit is made from 58.9 square inches of material. This is smaller than a single unfolded facial tissue.

Acne is frequently another reason going to the beach can be intimidating for some people. Clearasil has referred to acne as "face invaders." This commercial humiliates the person who has acne. Many teen magazines advertise these products knowing that they are reaching the teen market, and they are issues that teens are concerned about. Cosmetics are often used to make people feel more beautiful. But the irony is that "Some superrich moisturizers and heavy, oil-based makeup can aggravate acne."[11] According to *Dateline* (10/18/95) 30 billion dollars is spent each year on cosmetics.

Accomplishments and Abilities

The second most common area of comparison is with *Accomplishments and Abilities* (Judg. 8:2-3; Acts 8:19; Deut. 8:18).

Accomplishment competition occurs often among people. For example, when people are asked to describe themselves they usually begin with what job they have. If they don't value what they are doing with their life, they might use the words "only" or "just" before the description. This is a good indicator of mislocated esteem.

Comparing Ourselves to God

One of the first people in the Bible who had low self-esteem, because she compared herself to another was Eve. She compared herself to God and lost. Eve saw God on a regular basis, and she knew what he could do and had done. She also knew what she could do. She compared herself to God in abilities. Probably the ability that she compared most was God's ability to create the world and life. This is why Satan told her that she could become like God (Gen. 3:5). He thought this enticement would totally tempt her to eat the forbidden fruit and become something she really desired, becoming like God.

The problem was, she was already like God but she did not recognize it (Gen. 1:26-27). Woman can create life, and because she can do this, she is very much like God. Since she was made in God's image, that means they have much in common. The Hebrew word for "image" used here is *tselem*. It means image, likeness or resemblance. The root of this word means something cut out. This verse could actually say that God cut man out of his image. God was the pattern for the perfect creation of man. God traced himself to come up with the diagram and design for man.

God and man are alike in many ways. They both have emotions. They both can think. They both can create. They both make choices. They both know right from wrong. It could be that Adam and Eve did not recognize how much they were like God. This could be what Satan tapped into to tempt Adam and Eve to sin.

What would happen if you compared yourself to God? You would probably believe you were worthless. Philippians 2:7 declares that when God became a man, he made himself nothing. When you compare man to God, man looks like nothing. Even though man is something honored and valuable, when compared to God he **appears** to be as nothing. The Greek for "make . . . nothing" used here is *keno'o*. The word would better be defined as divesting himself of his privileges.

Comparing Ourselves to Bible Characters

But what would happen if you compared yourself to any Bible character? You would lose this comparison as well. Could a person compare themselves to Noah, Moses, Joshua, Gideon, David, Paul, and Peter and win the comparison? No way. You have never built an ark, led three million people out of bondage, destroyed a walled city, won a battle with 300 men, killed a giant, been talked to by God while you were traveling on a road, or walked on water. The above people did these activities and more.

Since you and I have not done these things, does this mean we are not as important or valuable to God? No! We are very valuable to God. He has not called us to do what he called these people to do. It is comparing ourselves to these and others that lowers our esteem. This is one of the reasons Paul says not to compare ourselves to someone else (Gal. 6:3-4).

I actually believe comparison is a sin since Satan tells us that by comparing ourselves to others we actually improve ourselves. There could be nothing that is farther from the truth than this. Satan wants us to compare ourselves so that we feel totally worthless, rotten and inferior to others. If these things happened, this would really please Satan and accomplish his goal of killing, stealing and destroying us.

Comparing Ourselves to Beauty

People consciously and subconsciously compare many things,

including beauty. Consider the results from an article in *Psychology Today* entitled "Beauty and the Best." It found that appearance can cause, determine or create many things:

☞ *grades are influenced by attractiveness*

☞ *unattractive children were selected as class troublemakers*

☞ *unattractive children were seen as more dishonest*

☞ *classroom discipline is often based on attractiveness*

☞ *some behaviors will be handled differently based on attractiveness*

☞ *the effects of physical attractiveness are established in nursery school*

Is this true also for adults, that people make judgments based on appearance? I believe people who are thin are seen as smarter and more successful. Heavy people are judged as being lazy and failures. Pauline Frederick said, "When a woman gets up to speak, people look; then if they like what they see, they listen." On June 16, 1995 ABC did a *20/20* segment about how pretty people are treated compared to average looking people. In one of the situations, *20/20* took two girls to downtown Atlanta and emptied their cars of gas. The average looking girl (dressed in the same outfit as the pretty one) did not have many people stop their cars, but she had several pedestrians stop and make suggestions about what *she* could do. It took almost 45 minutes before anyone got her some gas. The pretty girl had drivers not only stop to help her, some even had to back up to help her. At one time the video of this situation showed four or five males around her at one time. Lots of people offered to help. Before it was all over, she had her gas tank half filled.

The same program had two men and two women apply for similar jobs. The attractive male and female models were offered jobs more often, treated better in the interview, and given more money. The average models were told they would be called back, but they weren't. The attractive models were offered the jobs on the spot. The average models were not aware of this "discrimination" until after they talked with the attractive counterpart.

The show also took two actresses to a mall to raise money for a children's charity. They were going to sell items to raise the money. One of the actresses was pretty and the other one average. Both of them had people come by and donate to the charity, and it looked fairly even on number of donations. When they totaled the money raised, the average looking actress raised $60.00. The pretty actress raised $90.00, 50% more.

The same program went to a school and had two actresses pretend to be teachers. The first was of average appearance, the second one was prettier. Both teachers were in the same class at different times. They both taught similar material. In the first case the average teacher taught first. But in the second case the pretty teacher taught first. Then the kids were asked which one they liked best, which one was nicer, which one was smarter, and which one they would like to have as their teacher. The kindergarten kids chose the pretty teacher hands down.

Men usually compete to "gain" their esteem. Consider the following article about men competing and what it cost one man.

> CHATTANOOGA, Tenn. (AP) — Doctors failed to re-attach the hand that got torn off a man's wrist in a tug-of-war game at a company picnic.
>
> Stanley Dewane Farris, 21, was in fair condition Saturday in Erlanger Medical Center, hospital employee Doris Chastain said. She said "the injury was too severe" Friday to save the hand.
>
> Farris had rope wrapped around his wrist during the tug-of-war between teams of 25 adults. A hard tug by the other team severed his hand. Farris was his team's anchor, last in line.[13]

Why didn't this man let go so he could have saved his hand? Maybe he could not let go of the rope because of the way it was wrapped around his hand. It also could be because he did not want to lose the tug of war. Maybe he did not want to lose face (his esteem) in front of his friends.

Do you fall into these two traps? Do you value what the world does instead of what God values? Do you compare yourself to anybody and everybody? If the two reasons for low self-esteem we just discussed aren't enough, let's discuss eight other reasons in the next chapter.

Notes

1. *Good Housekeeping*, October 1995, p. 40.

2. Zig Ziglar, *See You at the Top* (Gretna, LA: Pelican Publishing Co., 1983).

3. *People* magazine, June 3, 1996, p. 71.

4. Joni Johnston, *Learning to Love the Way You Look*, p. 39.

5. Ibid., pp. 39-40.

6. Ibid., p. 40.

7. Ibid., p. 85.

8. "How tenny-weeny a bikini will American women wear?', *Muncie Evening Press*, 2/10/89.

9. Ibid.

10. Ibid.

11. *McCall's*, April 1995, p. 38.

12. *Psychology Today*, March 1972.

13. "Tennessee man loses hand in work picnic tug-of-war," *The Muncie Star*, Muncie, Indiana, June 11, 1995, p. 1.

5 Eight Other Reasons for Low Esteem

So far we have looked at the two major reasons for low self-esteem. But to say there are just two causes would be to minimize the scope of the problem. If there were only two causes, the problem would be fairly easy to correct. But Satan, the author of low esteem, has many schemes to attack Christians (1 Cor. 2:11).

There appear to be eight other reasons for the development of low self-esteem. These are not listed in any order of importance. All of these play a major part in the formation of low self-esteem.

Painful Past Events

This is one of the most common reasons for low self-esteem. Wounds and scars to a person's esteem develop from the past. It often takes years to undo what it took years to do. All of us know people who have been through painful past events. Many times they go through these events in secret, not telling anyone what has happened to them. There are many painful events that can dramatically affect a person's self-esteem.

- sexual abuse (incest, rape, molestation)
- pregnancy before marriage
- divorce of parents
- bad breakups of relationships
- infrequent dating
- abusive dating relationships
- rejection by peers
- criticism by significant people
- being ill and missing a lot of school
- having a physical, emotional or mental disability
- abortion
- premarital sex

Adultery has a profound effect on a person's self-esteem. Frequently the faithful spouse is going to compare him or herself to the paramour and lose. Adultery can also confirm and lower an already low esteem.

Unemployment and under-employment may also be events that lower esteem. Michael Holmes said, "As one of the unemployed, may I suggest that what we look for in our crisis is a spirit of discernment from those who come in touch with us. We don't want sympathy. Unemployment is a very personal and private thing. Don't try to understand it, or stand in judgment. . . . After all, unemployment is a traumatic and tender time for those who are its victims."

Divorce is another event that can lower a person's self-esteem. Tim Stafford wrote, "No one gets out completely unscarred. When people who have grown together are separated, it's never a simple, clean disconnection. It's like pulling a tree out of the ground—it's a violent act, and you can't do it without some damage."[1] Part of the damage occurs to the esteem of the children as well as to the esteem of the spouse who does not want the divorce.

Consider the following painful event that Alexandra Paul went through. (I have enclosed this for the humor in it.)

Actress talks about environment and jail

NEW YORK (AP)—The life of a "Baywatch" star isn't all sand and surf, Alexandra Paul says.

Her passion for protecting the environment has landed her behind bars. She said she has been arrested several times, once for protesting at a nuclear site in Nevada.

Of her jail time, Paul said, "I was only in there 4 ½ days, but when I got out, I had such low self-esteem. That's what jail does to you."[2]

It is frequently the consistent thinking about these painful past events and the blame we place on ourselves that lowers esteem. The Bible teaches that we should not dwell on past events (Isa. 43:18). Paul told people to forget "what is behind and strain toward what is ahead" (Phil. 3:13). One of the reasons for not dwelling on the past is that dwelling on the painful events hinders a person's self-esteem. Dennis and Barbara Rainey wrote, "Bitter memories of past failures can vandalize your mate's self-concept."[3] I like the word "vandalize" used here. Remember, I earlier called low self-esteem spiritual vandalism.

Fear of Others Being Better than Us

The fear that we are inferior to others has a component of not realizing that God is with you (Num. 14:9). Job had to deal with the threat of being inferior compared to his "friends." He realized that he was not inferior (Job 12:3; 13:2).

Fears are common with people who have low self-esteem. The fear of not being good enough is a common fear with low esteem people. This fear usually is created after a person has compared themselves to others and lost. These people may feel they are not attractive, so they become shy and easily embarrassed. They become shy because they feel that they have nothing to offer others. They feel awkward in new situations and do not like to be the center of attention. They frequently feel that if people really got to know them, they would not be liked.

Many people who have low self-esteem also have a fear of God abandoning them. This is what happened to Israel. They lost the perception that God was with them. This caused them to doubt themselves and their abilities. This is what created their low esteem. This is one of the attacks of Satan. He tried to get Jesus to doubt himself (Matt. 4:3, 6). He did this by saying to Jesus, "*If* you are the son of God . . ." (emphasis mine). He was hoping that Jesus doubted who he was and who was with him.

Childhood Events

Being a child can hurt self-esteem. Being a child on the playground can be a very devastating experience and can ruin esteem. Name-calling that occurs between children can have lasting effects on the individual even into adulthood. Many people feel about themselves today the way they did when they were in 5th grade. Bob George writes, "All of us carry the scars of past experiences. Just think of kids on the school playground, about how unkind they are to each other. Listen to all the nicknames: Porky, Rake, Dumbo, Stupid, Stinky, Pizza-face, Retardo. Think of the labeling: 'He's a slow learner.' . . . Many of us are still hurting and wrestling with those memories as we are becoming grandparents."[4]

Many social blunders can hurt esteem. For example, dropping your lunch tray in the cafeteria, being in a social situation with your zipper down, or kids making fun of you because of a speech impediment. When kids make fun of you because of these events, this greatly lowers esteem and confidence. If these events happen often enough or long enough, esteem can be destroyed for a lifetime. Besides the two situations mentioned above that can lower esteem, there are many others:

◆ parental abuse or neglect
◆ overbearing parental authorities
◆ parental response to the child (rejection, insulting, comparing).
◆ a home that did not tolerate mistakes

◆ parents who are aloof or uninvolved with their children. Psychologist Stanley Cooper in *The Antecedent of Self-Esteem* says the most significant characteristic to develop esteem in children is unconditional acceptance and love.[5] "Dr. Paul Roberts, the child psychologist, says that regular messages of acceptance and love are highly important in establishing a child's self-image."[6]

◆ parents who do not "defend" their children, but agree with the "attack" instead. It is important for a child to feel safe and protected when they are in the presence of their parents.

◆ parents who are gone often. Children frequently spell love "T-I-M-E." The more time you spend with them the more loved they feel. Time therefore is a crucial element in self-esteem.

◆ a home where worth and value were linked with the performance of the child. Recent studies show that there is a strong link between parental love and acceptance and self-esteem.

◆ younger siblings being compared to older ones.

◆ not being able to wear the same clothes as the other kids because of financial hardships — coming from "the wrong side of the tracks."

◆ repeatedly being chosen last in sporting activities — having "team captains" fight over not wanting you on their team.

◆ being raised by an alcoholic parent.

These are only some of the events that can occur in childhood that can hinder a person's esteem. It is important to recognize the connection between childhood events and painful past events and how they tie together to destroy esteem (1 Cor. 13:11).

Sin and Guilt

There are several verses which teach that sin will cause a person to loathe themselves. Ezekiel 20:43 says, "There you will remember your conduct and all the actions by which you have defiled yourselves, and you will loathe yourselves for all the evil you have done." Ezekiel 6:9 states, ". . . They will loathe themselves for the evil they have done and for all their detestable practices." Ezekiel 36:31 adds, ". . . and you will loathe yourselves for your sins and detestable practices."

Guilt devastates self-esteem. The prodigal son is a good example of this. In rehearsing his speech he was going to present to his father, he says that he is no longer worthy to be called a son (Luke 15:19). He actually said this to his father, but his father would not listen to it (Luke 15:21). His father quickly began to celebrate his son's return (Luke 15:22-24).

As a person is repeatedly reminded of the sins of the past, their esteem takes continual hits. Abortion is a good example of an event that can be repeatedly brought up that produces guilt, and lowers self-esteem. The final blow to the self may be the feeling of being worthless. Suicide and mental illness are not far from this point. Consider the following quote from Quentin Hyder M.D., "Guilt can cause someone to feel ugly when he is not, inadequate in any area of functioning when he in fact has great abilities, weak when he has great strength, or in any way inferior or unacceptable to others when in fact his friends and colleagues think highly of him."[7] What this doctor is saying is that guilt can create a 180-degree personality and behavioral turnaround. Consider the effects of sin and guilt on Adam and Eve.

Before Adam and Eve sinned they had no shame in being naked (Gen. 2:25). But after they sinned, they became ashamed of the way they looked (Gen. 3:7, 10). They knew they were naked, and they hid. I think Adam and Eve were also ashamed for what they had done. They hid because they could not face God since they had lost some of their value in their own eyes. It is interesting to think about the question, "How did Adam and Eve realize they were naked?" I believe that Satan is the one who told them with a wicked laugh. Satan had accomplished his goal at the time by getting man and woman kicked out of the garden, just like he had been kicked out of heaven. Satan lost his esteem when he was kicked out, and he assumed mankind would lose theirs as well. He did not expect man to be forgiven by God. He knew that God had not forgiven him. It will be discussed later that it is Calvary and its forgiveness that is the great event on which a person can and should build one's esteem.

It would be too general of a statement to say that all low esteem is because of sin and guilt. Bruce Parmenter wrote, "Low self-esteem is not always due to shame and guilt, but sometimes it is. Sometimes we depreciate ourselves because we deserve to be depreciated; we have done those things we should not have done and left undone what we should have done." He also wrote, "Low self-esteem can be, and frequently is, closely associated with an uneasy conscience."[8]

Even non-Christian books have made a connection between sin, guilt and low esteem. Richard A. Gardner, M.D. wrote, "Engaging in a sinful act produces feelings of low self-worth." He also wrote, "Central to guilt is low self-esteem."[9] It could be that these two strongholds (guilt and low self-esteem) actually form a vicious circle feeding off of each other. If this is true, it is easy to see why Satan would really like this.

I believe that Paul struggled with guilt. I believe this is one of the reasons he refers to himself as "the worst of sinners" (1 Tim. 1:13-16). Paul even referred to himself as the least of all apostles. He even stated that he did not deserve to be called an apostle (1 Cor. 15:9). What made Paul feel this way probably was the fact that he had killed Christians (Acts 7:54-8:1). This must have haunted him repeatedly. Anytime he came in contact with the children whose parents he had killed, this would cause him to feel guilty. This also would have lowered his esteem.

Faulty Personal Theology

Some ministers have even said that self-esteem is a sin and a teaching of the devil. Many verses in the Bible can be interpreted in such a way as to lower self-esteem. Some of these verses are

Romans 12:3; Matthew 5:5; Philippians 2:3-4; Isaiah 64:6; Leviticus 11:45; 19:2 to name only a few.

The NIV renders Galatians 6:3, "If anyone thinks he is something when he is nothing, he deceives himself." Could the opposite of this verse also be true: "If anyone thinks he is *nothing* when he is *something* he deceives himself"? I think that both of these deceptions are dangerous. It would be very easy for this verse to be interpreted to say "we are nothing." This has to have deadly consequences!

Philippians 2:3 in many translations can easily be misinterpreted and have lower esteem as the outcome. The Jerusalem Bible translates this verse, "There must not be any competition among you, no conceit; but everybody is to be self-effacing. Always consider the other person to be better than yourself, so that nobody thinks of his own interests first but everybody thinks of other people's interest instead." In the King James Version it reads, "Esteem others better than thyselves." Most people would interpret these verses as saying that other people are better than they. This means that you are worse than others. A better interpretation of this verse would be to say, "consider others *before* yourself." For your esteem to change, your faulty theology needs to be corrected. My favorite translation of this verse is found in the NASB. It reads, "Do nothing from selfishness or empty conceit, but with humility of mind let each of you regard one another as more important than himself." The word "regard" here means to *treat* others as more important than you. This is not saying that others *are* more important than you.

Another verse that is frequently misinterpreted is Romans 12:3, "For by the grace given me I say to everyone of you: Do not think of yourself more highly than you ought, but rather with sober judgment, in accordance with the measure of faith God has given you." People think that since we are taught we should not think of ourselves "too highly," we should think of ourselves as being lowly.

Many verses speak of people being lowly (Job 5:11; Psa. 119:141; 138:6; Prov. 16:19; 29:23; Isa. 57:15; Ezek. 21:26; 29:14; 1 Cor. 1:28; Phil. 3:21). The word "lowly" could be more accurately interpreted as humble. The New Testament uses the Greek word *tapeinos* for humble. The word can be described as a person's proper estimate of himself in relationship to God and others. The Old Testament words here are *anah* and *hapar* meaning "to bow down, submission."

Abraham Lincoln said, "It is difficult to make people miserable when they feel worthy of themselves." At times a person's personal theology makes him/her feel miserable and unworthy to enter the temple of God, to be blessed by God, or to be forgiven by God. No one is worthy of these things, but God declares people worthy. Paul writes in Romans 2:13, "For it is not the hearers of the law who are righteous in God's sight, but it is those who obey the law who will be declared righteous." In Acts 13:46 Paul is speaking to the Jews on the Sabbath about the issue of worth — "We had to speak the word of God to you first. Since you rejected it and do not consider yourselves worthy of eternal life, we now turn to the Gentiles."

The Bible does teach that several "kinds" of people are not allowed to enter the temple. In Deuteronomy 23 it gives four kinds of people who cannot enter the temple. The four are: those emasculated by crushing or cutting (23:1); those born of a forbidden marriage nor any of his descendants even down to the tenth generation; no Ammonite or Moabite or any of his descendants; and no Edomite until the third generation may enter the assembly of the Lord. The word "unworthy" is only found in the Bible four times in the NIV (Gen. 32:10; Job 40:4; Luke 17:10; 1 Cor. 11:27).

As I wrote at the beginning of this book, Satan is the author of low self-esteem. It is his teachings that cause a person to feel unworthy. The Greek word for Satan is "Satanas," meaning adversary, or one who resists. Satan would like all people to feel that God could not possibly love them or want them to go to heaven. Satan also teaches people that they are not true sons and daughters of God, but are illegitimate.

The truth is that God has no illegitimate children. For example in Hebrews, "If you are not disciplined (and everyone undergoes discipline), then you are illegitimate children and not true sons."

Satan will try to teach that many Christians are illegitimate and therefore have no right(s) to ask God for anything, or to even be in his presence. This is a bald-faced lie! The Hebrew word for "illegitimate" here is *mamzer*, meaning alien or mongrel. Hebrews 4:16 instructs us to "approach the throne of grace with confidence, so that we may receive mercy and find grace to help us in our time of need." Christians have "full rights of sons" (Gal. 4:5).

My favorite verse on our worth or worthiness is found in Hebrews 11:38 which states, "the world was not worthy of *them*. They wandered in deserts and mountains and in caves and holes in the ground." The word "them" is referring to the people mentioned in Hebrews 11 (the "Faith Hall of Fame"). People mentioned in this chapter are: Abel, Enoch, Abraham, Isaac, Jacob, Joseph, Moses, and Rahab to name only a few. Hebrews 11:32 says, "And what more shall I say? I do not have time to tell about Gideon, Barak, Samson, Jephthah, David, Samuel and the prophets." It is my belief that "them" also refers to Christians today. So this verse is talking about us!

To get a true perspective of self-esteem theology we need to turn to Jesus and his teaching. Jesus taught in Matthew 19:19, "Love your neighbor as yourself" (Matt. 22:39; Rom. 13:9). Jesus taught that if we don't love ourselves, we cannot love our neighbor the way we should. The question is then, do you love your neighbor as yourself? Probably not. We tend to love others much more than we love ourselves! Part of this lack of self-love is evident in the fact that there are people who are always wishing they could be somebody different.

Another teaching in the Bible is that all men are equal in the sight of God (Matt. 20:12; 23:8). Anthropologist Franz Boas said, "If we were to select the most intelligent, imaginative, energetic and emotionally stable third of all mankind, all races would be represented." Paul wrote in Colossians 3:11, "Here there is neither Greek or Jew, circumcised or uncircumcised, barbarian, Scythian, slave or free. But Christ is all and is in all." Jesus in Matthew 23:8 told the Pharisees, "But you are not to be called 'Rabbi,' for you have only one Master and you are all brothers." Both Jesus and Paul are stating that all people are equal. In Acts 17:26 we read, "And hath made of one blood all nations of men for to dwell on all the face of the earth and hath determined the times before appointed, and the bounds of their habitation" (KJV). This verse teaches that all nations of men have one blood.

The problem is that many people don't feel equal to others. Even Jesus' disciples did not feel equal to each other. They continually had a power struggle to figure out who the greatest disciple was. In fact, some felt superior to the others (Matt. 20:20-24; Mark 10:35-41). Jesus had to regularly deal with their inferiority and superiority attitudes (Luke 22:24). I think Paul addresses this in the letter he wrote the Philippians — "To all the saints in Christ Jesus at Philippi, together with the overseers and deacons" (1:1). He may have singled out the overseers and deacons because they may have thought this letter did not pertain to them.

Jesus taught much about self-esteem and self-adoration. He said, "the last will be first, and the first will be last" (Matt. 19:30; 20:16). This means that a person (one with good esteem—who feels good about himself) does not have to always be first. Young children frequently have a hard time with this concept. They want to be first in everything. Everything is a race and a form of competition. It is interesting to realize that what Jesus taught here and what the world believes are completely different (Isa. 55:8-9).

Jesus taught, "whoever wants to become the greatest among you must be your servant, and whoever wants to be first must be your slave" (Matt. 20:26-27; 23:11). Jesus was teaching the disciples a different way of looking at greatness. Great people are workers in the kingdom of God.

Satan and His Lies

Jesus refers to Satan as a liar and the Father of lies (John 8:44-45). Paul when he wrote to Timothy said that Satan is a teacher who will prompt people to abandon the faith by the doctrines he teaches (1 Tim. 4:1). Peter writes that Satan is a roaring lion seeking people he can destroy (1 Peter 5:8). Paul writes that Satan blinds minds (2 Cor. 4:4). The goals of the devil are to oppress Christians, to kill, steal and destroy them (Dan. 7:25; John 10:10). Satan has many avenues in which to teach his lies.

Neil Anderson and Steve Russo write, "Satan's greatest weapons for confusing our kids in relation to their identity are his lies."[10] Ephesians 6:12 reports that we "wrestle" with the Devil. The Greek word *pale* is used here. It means "to sway." This could mean that the devil wants to sway us to believe his opinion about us.

Satan's lies about low self-esteem are taught! They are taught in a wide variety of ways. They come from society, media and from "teachers." "The elders and prominent men are the head, the prophets who teach lies are the tail" (Isa. 9:15). The lies we believe can become part of a person's theology. Isaiah 28:15b states, "for we have made a lie our refuge and falsehood our hiding place." People believe the lie of low esteem so well that when others disagree with their opinion of themselves, they think they are lying.

Some of the lies people believe about themselves are:

I'm worthless.

I'm under a curse.

Nothing I attempt to accomplish ever turns out.

If you knew me, you would not like me.

You're better than me.

I'm ugly.

Zechariah 3:1 pictures Satan at mankind's right hand making accusations. It is believing these accusations (which are cleverly disguised lies) that lowers esteem. We believe the lies so fully, that when people disagree with our negative opinion of ourselves, we think they are lying.

The Living Bible gives an interesting paraphrase of what Paul wrote to the church at Rome. "As God's messenger I give each of you God's warning: Be honest in your estimate of yourselves, measuring your value by how much faith God has given you" (Rom. 12:3). It is very difficult to be honest in our estimation of ourselves when the Devil is constantly lying to us about our worth to God. Neil Anderson and Steve Russo write, "If our children don't understand their worth in Christ, the enemy will try and convince them that they are worthless. And when a child thinks he's worthless he will behave as if he is worthless, bringing destruction to himself and to his family. . . ."[11]

What were the first two temptations of Jesus by Satan? In Matthew 4:1-11 Jesus deals with Satan, who attempts to make Jesus verbalize his identity. Twice he said to him, "*if* you are the Son of God . . . ." Satan knew who Jesus was. He knew that if Jesus did not know who he was, he would not be effective in his ministry. Satan also tried to get Eve to prove who she was to him. Satan told her in Genesis 3:1, "You surely will not die. For God knows that when you eat of it your eyes will be opened, and you will be like God, knowing good and evil." Eve did not realize a very important fact – she and Adam were already like God (Gen. 1:26-27). These temptations were also designed to get Jesus and Adam and Eve to depend on themselves for their needs and not on God.

God has given us the truth to expose and resist the lies of the devil. Jesus said in John 8:32, "You shall know the truth and the truth will set you free." If we find out the truth of who we are, then the Satanic bondage of low self-esteem is broken. Jesus prayed about this bondage and the devil. In John 17:15, "My prayer is not that you take them out of the world but that you protect them from the evil one." In verse 17, "Sanctify them by the truth; your word is truth." Paul tells us to put on the "belt of truth" (Eph. 6:14). I believe that the only source of identity and truth about who man is and the value of man is found in the Bible!

What We Watch, Listen to, and Read

Proverbs 4:23 encourages, "Above all else, guard your heart, for it is the wellspring of life." Matthew 6:22-23 affirms, "The eye is the lamp of the body. If the eyes are good, your whole body will be full of light. But if your eyes are bad, your whole body will be full of darkness. If then the light within you is darkness, how great is that darkness." One of the dangers is that what we watch, we want to become. This causes great darkness. Many people compare themselves to the models and actresses they see on the TV. Consider the following quote:

A 39-year-old female accountant said, "When I think about my appearance in comparison to the women in the magazines and on TV, I feel insecure and have low self-esteem. Then I get angry at myself for feeling insecure and having low self-esteem." It is comparison that the media is hoping for. This causes people to want to buy the products they sell to enhance a person's appearance. This makes money, big money for the media.

What does the media esteem in people that would make the above individual have low self-esteem? Beauty and riches. The media teaches that you need a body by Fisher (the company that makes automobile bodies) and brains by Mattel! The typical "airhead" is what comes to mind here. In his book, *Hide and Seek*, James Dobson identifies two powerful artificial value systems in our society: beauty and intelligence.[12] Many TV shows have nothing but people that match this image. *Beverly Hills 90210*, *Models Inc.*, and *Baywatch* are only some of these wonderful examples. For those of us who are from the '70s it was shows like the *Love Boat* and *Fantasy Island*.

One of the movies to be recently released was the Disney cartoon *Pocahontas*. Bob Smithouser writes in Parental Guidance, "To begin with, instead of a modest 12-year-old *historical* figure, Disney vied for a fully mature *hourglass* figure. A nubile native. This pen-and-ink Powhatan princess presents an unattainable standard of beauty. Glen Keane supervised that animation of the character. He said, 'We're doing a mature love story here, and we've got to draw her as such. She has got to be sexy. . . . This is not a documentary.' No kidding. Have you examined his artwork? Before impressionable young girls attempt to achieve that Pocahontas 'look' (and develop an eating disorder in the process), you may want to point out that no woman with a full set of ribs and internal organs can pull it off."[13]

There are some interesting results about the media and self-esteem. Joni Johnston writes, "the women's magazines contain 10.5 times more articles related to dieting and weight loss than did the men's magazines." She also reported that a study of *Playboy* centerfolds and Miss America contestants measurements from 1979 to 1988, "found that the majority of women had a body weight 13 percent to 19 percent below the normal weight for women in that age group." Also, "Sixty-nine percent of female television characters are thin, and only 5 percent are overweight."[14]

Men are not immune from the media's attack on their self-esteem. Joni Johnston observes four things about men and the media.

1. When comparing men's magazines to women's magazines, men's magazines have a disproportionate number of articles that address the idea of body shaping.

2. The "average" size of the models and mannequins have become more muscular and fit. The new mannequins are 6'2" and have a 42" chest and need a size 42 suit. The old mannequins used to be size 38.

3. The diet industry is going after men more by using sport celebrities. *SlimFast* (which is a great name for a diet aide) has recruited people like Tommy LaSorda, the manager of the Los Angeles Dodgers.

4. Men spend approximately 2 million dollars a year for hair replacements and medical treatments for hair loss.[15]

What does the media not esteem? Overweight, ugly, poor people to name only a few traits. These people are frequently treated like they are nerds, and unproductive to our society. The danger here is that the ideas taught in the media become the ideas of the society.

The media outright lies about the body images of many popular actresses and actors. The media knows people cannot compete with an airbrushed (touched up) photograph. The media knows no one looks like the girls on the magazine cover . . . not even the girl on the cover. The media also knows an average person can't compete with the plastic surgeon's knife and skill.

Joni Johnston wrote, "Plastic surgery tripled between 1986 and 1988; 80 percent of the surgeries were for cosmetic reasons."[16] She also stated that women account for 75 percent of all surgeries. Why is there so much interest in plastic surgery? Part of the reason lies in the fact that so many people are dissatisfied with the way they look. They believe that if they looked better things would probably go better. Plastic surgery can become addictive, where people want to do it more and more.

Why does the media use skinny people in diet commercials? So we will compare ourselves to them and so they can teach us "I'm skinny, I'm on a diet. Look at you! You should be on a diet!" How does the media portray thin people? (Competent, have all the fun, successful, attractive, smart, popular, more professional, outgoing, and having a sense of humor).

The People We Are Around (Our Society)

Proverbs 22:24-25 states that we should not make friends with a hot tempered man because we could learn his ways and become ensnared. The same thing happens to us when we are around people who have low self-esteem. If we are around them, we can learn their ways. Deuteronomy 20:8 states, "Then the officers shall add, 'Is any man afraid or faint-hearted? Let him go home so that his brothers will not become disheartened too." Low esteem, like fear, can be learned from the people you are around. Paul wrote in 1 Corinthians 15:33, "Do not be deceived, bad company corrupts good character." Bad company can corrupt a person's self-esteem. For example, if you are continually around people that put you down, you will become down on yourself. It is important for people to be very careful about who they hang around with. Proverbs 12:26 states, "A righteous man is cautious in friendship, but the way of the wicked lead them astray."

What is frequently the hidden agenda of low or wrong self-esteem (Luke 6:26)? Bill Cosby said, "I don't know the key to success, but the key to failure is trying to please everyone." We want all people to like and speak well of us. When they don't do both of these things this lowers our esteem. According to Luke 6:22 what are four things people are going to do to us if we are Christians?

1. Hate us
2. Exclude us
3. Reject us
4. Insult us

"I want everyone to like me." This is a common plea from many people. This will never happen. First of all you don't know everyone. And secondly, the Bible teaches that all men are going to hate Christians because of Christ (Matt. 10:22; Mark 13:13). What does Matthew 10:22 and Proverbs 29:10, 27 tell us that people are going to do to Christians? Matthew 10:22 teaches us that the world is going to hate us because of Jesus. Proverbs 19:10 teaches us that people of integrity are hated by bloodthirsty men, and they will seek to kill the upright. Proverbs 29:27 teaches that the wicked will detest the upright, and the righteous will detest the dishonest. So if we are relying on the world to build up our esteem — it will not happen!

It is ironic, but some of our teachers of esteem are our parents (Ezek. 16:44). High self-esteem has been linked to strong disciplinary parents who are not harsh, and who have a strong love for their children. W. Hugh Missildine wrote, "A child develops his sense of being a worthwhile, capable, important, and unique individual from the attention given him by his parents."[17] The idea that "key people" influence one's self-esteem is not new. Janet Harrell and Carl A. Ridley found that "Babies need the mother's devoted and constant care in order to develop the emotional security that underlies a strong concept of self."[18]

Esau is a great example of a person wanting to receive parental acceptance and encouragement. Esau felt a great desire to be blessed by his father. Genesis 27:34 records, "When Esau heard his father's words, he burst out with a loud and bitter cry and said to his father, 'Bless me — me too, my father!'" In Genesis 27:38, "Esau said to his father, 'Do you have only one blessing, my father? Bless me too, my father!' Then Esau wept aloud." He was so upset with his twin brother for stealing the blessing that he thought about killing him (Gen. 27:41). The blessing Esau wanted from his father was an affirmation of worth and value. It was important because it would affect him for the rest of his life. It was a prediction or prophesy about what his life would hold for him.

The idea of a blessing is very common in the Bible. The first blessing in the Bible came from God to Abram. "I will make you into a great nation and I will bless you; I will make your name great, and you will be blessed. I will bless those who bless you, and whoever curses you I will curse, and all peoples on earth will be blessed through you" (Gen. 12:2-3).

Not everyone received a positive blessing in the Bible. Jacob blessed all twelve of his sons in Genesis 49, but they did not receive equal blessings. For instance, "Zebulun will live by the seashore and become a haven for ships; his border will extend toward Sidon. Issachar is a rawboned donkey lying down between two saddlebags. When he sees how good his resting place and how pleasant is his land, he will bend his shoulders to the burden and submit to forced labor."

Some of the twelve tribes received mixed blessings from their father Jacob. The blessings Jacob gave his other sons are:

Reuben, "you will no longer excel" (Gen. 49:4).

Simeon and Levi, "Cursed be their anger, so fierce, and their fury, so cruel! I will scatter them in Jacob and disperse them in Israel" (Gen. 49:7).

Judah, "Your brothers will praise you; your hand will be on the neck of your enemies; your father's sons will bow down to you" (Gen. 49:7).

Dan, "Will provide justice for his people as one of the tribes of Israel. Dan will be a serpent by the roadside, a viper along the path, that bites the horse's heels so that its rider tumbles backward" (Gen. 49:16-17).

Gad, "Will be attacked by a band of raiders, but he will attack them at their heels" (Gen. 49:19).

Asher, "Asher's food is rich; he will provide delicacies fit for a king" (Gen. 49:20).

Naphtali, "Naphtali is a doe set free that bears beautiful fawns" (Gen. 49:21).

Joseph, "Joseph is a fruitful vine" (Gen. 49:21). "Because of your father's God, who helps you, because of the Almighty, who blesses you with blessings of the heavens above, blessings of the deep that lies below, blessings of the breast and womb" (Gen. 49:25).

Benjamin, "Benjamin is a ravenous wolf; in the morning he devours the prey, in the evening he divides the plunder" (Gen. 49:27).

The blessing is something that can be given to our children today. Gary Smalley writes in *The Blessing* that there are five basic parts of the family blessing.

1. The meaningful touch.
2. The spoken message.
3. Attaching "high value" to the One being blessed.
4. Picturing a special future for the One being blessed.
5. An active commitment to fulfilling the blessing.[19]

Have you been blessed recently? If not, which of the eight areas we just discussed trouble you the most? These areas result in visible symptoms of low self-esteem. There may be signs that you, or someone you love, are dealing with inappropriate esteem. We will discuss several of these signs in the next chapter.

Notes

1. Tim Stafford, *Love, Sex and the Whole Person.*

2. *The Evening Press*, Thursday, August 10, 1995, p. 17.

3. Dennis and Barbara Rainey, *Building your Mate's Self-Esteem* (San Bernardino, CA: Here's Life Publishers, 1990), p. 94.

4. Bob George, *Classic Christianity.*

5. Stanley Coopersmith, *The Antecedents of Self-Esteem* (San Francisco: W.H. Freeman, 1967), p. 165.

6. Alan Loy McGinnis, *The Friendship Factor* (Minneapolis: Augsburg Publishing House, 1979), p. 98.

7. O. Quentin Hyder, *The Christian's Handbook of Psychiatry* (Old Tappan, NJ: Revell, 1971), p. 114.

8. Bruce Parmenter, *What the Bible Says about Self-Esteem*, pp. 32, 31.

9. Richard A. Gardner, M.D., *Self-Esteem Problems of Children* (Cresskill, NJ: Creative Therapeutics, 1992), pp. 351, 354.

10. Neil Anderson and Steve Russo, *The Seduction of Our Children* (Eugene, OR: Harvest House Publishers, 1991), p. 20.

11. Ibid., p. 17.

12. James Dobson, *Hide and Seek* (Old Tappan, NJ: Revell, 1974).

13. Bob Smithouser writes in *Parental Guidance*, August 15, 1995, Vol. 6, No. 2 from *Focus on the Family*.

14. Joni Johnston, *Learning to Love the Way You Look*, p. 39.

15. Ibid., p. 43.

16. Ibid., p. 40.

17. W. Hugh Missildine, *Your Inner Child of the Past* (New York: Simon and Schuster, 1963), p. 37.

18. Harold W. Bernard, *Human Development in Western Culture*, 5th edition (Boston: Allyn and Bacon, Inc., 1978), p. 522.

19. Gary Smalley, *The Blessing* (Nashville: Thomas Nelson Publishers, 1986), p. 24.

6 Signs of Low Self-Esteem

How common is low esteem? James Dobson said, "Many men feel as insecure and worthless as do similarly troubled members of the gentle sex. In fact, low self-esteem is a threat to the entire human family, affecting children, adolescents, the elderly, all socio-economic levels of society, and each race and culture. It can engulf anyone who feels disrespect in the eyes of other people."

A List of Low Esteem Signs

If a person was to identify signs of low esteem, what would he or she be looking for? Below is a list of some of the signs of low self-esteem.

◆ Fear of expressing and receiving anger. Low esteem people believe that if they express anger, they will be rejected. They also believe that if people are angry at them, they are rejecting them.
◆ lying to enhance self-importance
◆ self-negating verbally
◆ difficulty admitting wrong, has a need to always be right
◆ expressions of shame and guilt are frequent. Mellody Beaty

wrote, "We feel so bad about ourselves and have such a need to be perfect and avoid shame that we cannot allow anyone to tell us about something we're doing wrong. One reason some of us nag and criticize other people is because that's what we do to ourselves."[1]

◆ constantly apologizes
◆ rationalizes away positive comments about self (seen as lies)
◆ exaggerates negative comments about self (seen as truth)
◆ afraid to try new things
◆ eye contact poor
◆ overly compliant to others
◆ peace at all cost with people. Frequently saying "yes" when they want to say "no."
◆ constantly seeking reassurance from others about what they are doing or saying
◆ self-destructive behavior
◆ constantly asking people if they are angry or mad at you
◆ perfectionism
◆ avoidance of possible failure situations
◆ angered easily, but it is usually expressed internally
◆ low or loss of motivation
◆ chemical dependency
◆ passivity
◆ feeling inferior to others
◆ self-pity, easily discouraged by others or events
◆ expectation and exaggeration of rejection
◆ hopes not allowed to become a reality
◆ belief that people really don't care about them
◆ despising personal appearance
◆ opinions on topics frequently change to match environment and people, lacks confidence in their own decision making
◆ intimidating, bullying and critical of others
◆ jealousy
◆ low esteem people tend to be more easily persuaded than high esteem people.

Dr. G. Keith Olson, in his book *Why Teenagers Act the Way They Do*, gives eight personality types of adolescents. One of the types he labels as the "Self-Demeaning" personality. He says that this is a submissive type of personality. Dr. Olson writes, "A self-demeaning teenager prefers people who will reinforce self-depreciating feelings. As he or she assumes the role of clown or buffoon, others respond with laughter and demeaning responses. These reactions are particularly intense when others are convinced this adolescent really is inept, foolish, clumsy and inferior."[2]

Dr. Olson wrote, "Self-demeaning adolescents are convinced they are weak and incompetent. They feel inadequate to live life effectively. They believe they are unworthy of meaningful relationships."[3]

Ecclesiastes 5:17 gives three very frequent signs of low self-esteem:

1. great frustration
2. affliction
3. anger.

The reason they eat alone in the dark is so that no one will get to know them and later reject them. In other words, they are shy because of fear.

Joshua 10:24 describes a common trait of low esteem people. They will let people put them down and step on them without defending themselves. They never have a comeback to criticism. They accept it as truth. They are afraid to make people mad. They see anger as being a form of rejection.

Job had to deal with the idea of being "inferior" to his three friends who were attacking him about his losses. In Job 12:3 he protests, "But I have a mind as well as you; I am not inferior to you. Who does not know all these things?" In Job 13:2 he continues, "What you know, I also know; I am not inferior to you." If Job had low self-esteem he could not have said these things to defend himself.

Symptoms of Inferiority

In *The Psychology of Abnormal Behavior,* Barney Katz and Louis P. Thorpe list the following symptoms that would indicate the presence of a rather pronounced degree of inferiority feelings:

Seclusiveness: the individual avoids being with other people, refuses to participate in social activities and seeks to be alone.

Self-Consciousness: the individual is reserved and easily upset in the presence of others.

Sensitivity: the individual is especially sensitive to criticism or unfavorable comparison with other people.

Projection: the individual blames and criticizes others, seeing in them the traits or motives which he feels to be unworthy in himself.

Ideas of Reference: the individual applies to himself all unfavorable remarks as well as criticisms made by others.

Attention-Getting: the individual endeavors to attract attention by any method that seems likely to be successful; he attempts to gain notice by crude devices that are usually not socially rewarding.

Dominating: the individual endeavors to govern others, usually smaller and younger persons, by bullying and brow-beating them.

Compensation: the individual covers up or disguises his inferiority by exaggeration of a desirable tendency or trait, sometimes in a socially acceptable manner and sometimes in a socially disapproved or anti-social one.[4]

One of the most common signs found in people with low self-esteem is the belief that they are not equal to others. Is it true that all men are not created equal? In 1 Samuel 9:2 Saul was described as, "an impressive young man without equal among the Israelites — a head taller than any of the others." In 1 Kings 3:13 God tells Solomon, "Moreover, I will give you what you have not asked for — both riches and honor — so that in your lifetime you will have no equal among kings." Yet in Matthew 20:12 Jesus tells a parable that depicts equal treatment by God.

Four Signs of Wrong Self-Eseem

What are four significant signs of wrong self-esteem? It is ironic, but of the four I list as significant signs of wrong self-esteem, the world considers the first three to be almost normal. This is because our world has become almost immune to low self-esteem.

Cohabitation

Living together without being married is a sign of low self-esteem. Cohabitation rates have soared since the 1970s, when only 11% of those marrying lived together before marriage, to 67% in the 1990s, reports the University of Wisconsin's National Survey on Families and Households.

Bulimia, anorexia nervosa

Eating disorders is the second sign of low self-esteem. Bulimia is a binging and purging sequence. They will eat large amounts of food and then self-induce vomiting or use laxatives. Some estimate that 50% of college females have done this sequence at least some of the time. Research done by A.J. Stunkard in 1987 said that true bulimics, those that do it on a regular basis, are less than 2% of the college females.[5]

Anorexia is self-starvation for the goal of thinness. Karen Carpenter, a popular singer in the '70s and '80s, died of it. The most common group for anorexia is females in adolescence and early adulthood, from middle and upper income families who are well educated. Research shows that only about 5% of anorexics are males.

Eating disorders have been around for years. Consider the following article in the *New York Times*. "Thousands of young girls in schools, colleges and offices are not dieting, as they fondly believe, but are starving themselves . . . the modern girl . . . is so afraid of being overweight that she is not willing to be even normal weight."[6]

Does it surprise you that this was written in 1926? It should not. Ecclesiastes 1:9 reminds us, "What has been will be again, what has been done will be done again; there is nothing new under the sun." By the way, we have been lied to when society has been taught by psychology that bulimia, anorexia and pica are diseases. They are very simply signs of low self-esteem.

Quentin Hyder, M.D. wrote, "Frustration, *poor self-image*, hostility, resentment, and depression are all neurotic problems related to the tendency to overeat."[7] It could be that overeating is a form of punishment people want to inflict upon themselves.

How common are eating disorders? A Stanford University survey of 1728 California sophomores found that 13 percent occasionally try to lose weight by vomiting or using laxatives or diuretics, which alter body fluid levels. Girls who try it outnumber boys 2-1. Joel D. Killen, Ph.D, of Stanford University Medical School's Center for Research and Disease Prevention, surveyed 1,728 sophomores from four California High Schools. He found that one out of eight had tried vomiting or consumed laxatives or other drugs to lose weight. Twice as many girls as boys tried this.[8]

Why would people use such severe methods to lose weight? The attitudes towards body weight, shape and the use of dieting and other weight control practices has been the subject of many studies. In one study using 854 females, 12-23, the results showed that more than 50% of the females did not like their body shape and 38% had attempted to lose weight by dieting. 67% were dissatisfied with their weight. Only 53% were higher or lower than the normal weight levels. Fasting and other extreme measures for losing weight were the most prevalent among the high school age group.

Since 1979 a majority of contestants of the Miss America pageant are 15% below the recommended weight for their height.[9] Being below your body weight by this percentage is one of the symptoms of anorexia nervosa. According to the American Psychiatric Association, since 1970 the incidence of bulimia and anorexia has doubled.

Premarital sexual activity

Promiscuity is the third symptom of low self-esteem. Low esteem people frequently believe that if the people they are dating do not want sex with them, they must not like them. So their dates wanting sex with them "proves" they like or love them.

Low esteem people also believe that people can treat them "too good." How can someone treat you too good? Low esteem people are not used to being treated nicely, and so something must be wrong with the relationship if they are. Satan teaches this philosophy.

The media has done a lot to hype sexuality and self-esteem. Recently Cindy Crawford did an interview with *USA Today*, where she was reacting to a segment about *children and sex* on ABC TV's *Prime Time Live*. She said, "I can't believe that a 10-year-old boy was shaking my exercise video and singing (she mimics): 'Take off that swimsuit!' It was a sad thing because of what it means for little girls — that 'being sexy' — was the way they had to get men. It's tough. I'm in an industry which kind of gives these images. . . . Part of that is the responsibility of the parents, but part of it is ours."[10]

Much has been written about promiscuity. Josh McDowell wrote, "Thus, the childhood need for fatherly affection is the root cause behind the sexual promiscuity of many young women today."[11] I do not hold to this idea very firmly. I believe that many girls give into sexual pressures from their boyfriends because they don't want to lose them. Sex is seen and used as a way of keeping the relationship going. Richard A. Gardner, M.D. wrote,

> If a girl is promiscuous, i.e., she indiscriminately engages in sex with a large number of boys, there is generally a pathological problem operative. Often it relates to the feeling of low self-worth and the feeling that she could not attract boys without providing them with sex. I try to help such girls appreciate that they are humiliating themselves and that the lack of respect the boys have for them because of their promiscuity is likely to diminish even further their feelings of low self-worth.[12]

Low esteem people are more likely to have premarital sex because they put their esteem in their relationships. If the relationship ends, their esteem ends. There are some people who will do anything to keep a relationship going. Low esteem people have the faulty belief that **any** relationship is better than no relationship.

There is a strong connection between the media and premarital sexual activity. The *AFA Journal* (October 1993) reported on a study about the amount of sexual activity on television. This article said that 86% of all sex presented on prime-time programming on ABC, CBS, and NBC is depicted outside of marriage. This study analyzed television from May 2, 1993 to May 29, 1993.

Teen Sexual Activity Rises. In the 1980s, sexual activity among teenage girls — particularly those from white upper and middle income families — rose sharply in this country. So shows a recent study published in Family Planning Perspectives. The study, conducted by researchers from The Alan Guttmacher Institute, is based on data from 8000 women aged 15-44. The data shows that:

> The percentage of girls aged 15 to 19 who reported engaging in sexual activities increased from 47.1% in 1982 to 53.2% in 1988.
> The percentage of sexually active girls in the 15 to 17 year old age bracket rose from 32.6% to 38.4% in the same period.
> In 1988, 58% of sexually active teenage girls reported having two or more sex partners.
> In 1982, 48% of the sexually active girls age 15 to 19 reported that contraceptives were used in their first sexual intercourse. In 1988, 65% of the girls 15 to 19 reported that contraceptives, mostly condoms, were used in their first sexual intercourse.

Promiscuity not only is a sign of low self-esteem but it is also a worldly way to build esteem. I have known people who want to sleep with as many people as they possibly can. This is true with both guys and girls. I have known females who enjoy guys making passes at them. They enjoy dressing provocatively to attract attention. I have known guys who enjoy having as many female sexual partners as they can attain and brag about it.

The two most recent and prolific braggers of the numbers of

sexual partners would be Gene Simmons of the rock group Kiss and Wilt Chamberlain. Chamberlain bragged about being with 20,000 women. If I am not mistaken I think Gene Simmons has said he had been with over 3000 women. A recent Jerry Springer show had a woman as a guest who I think had slept with 251 men in a ten hour period. Is this something to be really proud of and tell your grandchildren?

Girls can build their esteem on guys' comments and come ons. This type of behavior to gain esteem will eventually lead to death. "There is a way that seems right to a man, but in the end it leads to death" (Prov. 16:25). A good case in point here is Magic Johnson.

Suicide

Let it be enough for me to state here that the rate of teenage suicide has more than tripled since 1960. This statistic has a strong correlation with the increase in divorce which has quadrupled over the same period. Could divorce cause an increase in the suicide rate, and also lower self-esteem? I believe the answer is most definitely yes! Marjorie Toomin wrote, "In divorce children lose a psychological support system."[13] It is my belief that girls of divorcees have lower self-esteem, than girls who come from two parent families.

Newsweek reported that there is one divorce every 27 seconds.[14] Grace Ketterman, M.D. wrote, "A colleague of mine has studied the families of multiply handicapped children for some years. Despite the most careful counsel, expert medical help, and the building of a support system, there is a tragically high divorce rate among these families."[15] In these situations, the chance for children with low esteem has got to be greatly increased, because of the handicap and the divorce.

In 1990, 30% of all children were living with only one parent. In Marion County, Indiana (which includes the city of Indianapolis), there were 7000 divorces in 1991. Sixty to seventy percent of those divorcing had children under the age of 18. Recent figures by the Census Bureau show that the percentage of American adults who have been divorced more than tripled between 1970 and 1990.

Since 1972 more than one million children have been newly affected by divorce each year according to the Center for Health Statistics. It is estimated that 45% of all children born in any given year will live with only one of their parents at some time before they are 18. Approximately 60% of people divorcing have children.

Ernest Bruder wrote about the connection of suicide and self-esteem when he stated, "One is greatly tempted here to consider suicide as the most extreme manifestation of the feeling of personal unworthiness. One hears so frequently from suicidal people the phrase, 'I'm not fit to live with.' It's a phrase which in itself has most meaningful implications. Certainly we can see in such people the final evidences of complete loss of self-esteem."[16]

Did you see yourself, or someone you love, in any of these symptoms? If so, you are not alone. People in the Bible dealt with these same problems. They came in all shapes and sizes. They may have had too high esteem, low esteem, or correct esteem. I'll profile a few of these people, and look at how their esteem affected their lives.

Notes

1. Mellody Beaty, *Co-dependent No More* (New York: Harper and Row, 1992).

2. Dr. G. Keith Olson, *Why Teenagers Act the Way They Do* (Loveland, CO: Group Books, 1987), p. 260.

3. Ibid., pp. 276-277.

4. Barney Katz and Louis P. Thorpe, *The Psychology of Abnormal Behavior* (The Ronald Press, 1948).

5. A. J. Stunkard, *Eating Regulation and Discontrol* (Hillsdale, NJ: Erlbaum).

6. *New York Times*, October 12, 1926.

7. O. Quentin Hyder, *The Christian's Handbook of Psychiatry* (Old Tappan, NJ: Revell, 1971), p. 129.

8. *USA Today*, March 21, 1986.

9. *People* magazine, June 3, 1996, p. 67.

10. *USA Today*, May 17, 1995.

11. Josh McDowell, *His Image . . . My Image* (San Bernardino, CA: Here's Life Publishers, Inc., 1984), p. 81.

12. Richard A. Gardner, M.D., *Self-Esteem Problems of Children* (Cresskill, NJ: Creative Therapeutics, 1992), p. 339.

13. Marjorie Toomin, *Counseling Needs of Children of Divorce.*

14. David Gelman et al., "Playing Both Mother and Father," *Newsweek*, July 15, 1985.

15. Grace H. Ketterman, M.D., *You and Your Child's Problems* (Old Tappan, NJ: Revell), p. 47.

16. Ernest E. Bruder, *Ministering to Deeply Troubled People* (Englewood Cliffs, NJ: Prentice-Hall, Inc., 1963), p. 88.

7 Profiles of Esteem in the Bible

Those Whose Esteem Was Too High

It must be emphasized that good self-esteem is like balancing a teeter-totter. If esteem gets too low that is dangerous. If esteem gets too high this too is dangerous. What would you call too high esteem? Arrogance, conceit?

Psalm 10:2 puts it like this: "In his arrogance the wicked man hunts down the weak, who are caught in the schemes he devises." Who were some people in the Bible who had too high self-esteem? How many people fit this description? I have found several.

King Herod (Acts 12:21-23). He refused to give God praise so he was eaten by worms and died.

Religious leaders (Matt. 23:5-7; Luke 18:9-14). These people had too high esteem to associate with the "sinners" of the world. Jesus confronts them about their behaviors and beliefs in Matthew 23.

Uzziah (2 Chron. 26:16). After this king became powerful, his pride led to his downfall and he was unfaithful to the Lord. It could be emphasized here that people who have too high self-esteem frequently have no room or no perceived need for God in their lives. This man was sixteen years old when he became king and he reigned for fifty-two years. It could have been his success at such an early age that led to his prideful downfall. Psalm 10:4 states, "In his pride the wicked does not seek him; in all his thoughts there is no room for God."

Nebuchadnezzar (Dan. 5:18-21). It says in verse 20, "But when his heart became arrogant and hardened with pride, he was deposed from his royal throne and stripped of his glory." It was his pride and arrogance (two signs of too high esteem) that cost him his kingdom.

Belshazzar (Dan. 5:22-23). He was the son of Nebuchadnezzar who knew what happened to his father, yet he refused to humble himself. Verse 23 states, "Instead, you have set yourself up against the God of Heaven." Too high esteem could actually be the cause of a person's downfall because they set themselves up against God.

The kings of Babylon and Tyre (Isa. 14:11-15; Ezek. 28:11-17). Some people think these passages refer to Satan as the greatest angel who wanted to rise above God, his creator. This desire is what eventually sent him to hell.

Jacob (Israel) (Amos 6:8). This passage states that God abhors pride.

Assyria (Zech. 10:11). It was Assyria's pride that led to her downfall. This correlates to Proverbs 18:12, "Before his downfall a man's heart is proud."

The disciples (Matt. 18:1). What question did the disciples ask Jesus one day? *Who is the greatest*? What answer do you think they were hoping to hear? Each was hoping to hear his own name! The disciples continually argued about who was the greatest (Mark 9:34; Luke 9:46; 22:24).

What did James and John ask Jesus to do for them (Mark 10:35-40)? To allow them to sit at Jesus' right and left hand in heaven. How did their mother get involved with the debate (Matt. 20:20-28)? She had the same request they did.

Having too high esteem prompts people to become self-exalting. There are many examples of self-exaltation in Scripture. The following is a partial list, some of which have been covered in detail above.

Pharaoh	Exodus 9:18
Korah, Dathan and Abiram	Numbers 16:1-3
Sennacherib	2 Chronicles 32:9-19
Prince of Tyre	Ezekiel 28:2, 9
Nebuchadnezzar	Daniel 4:30; 5:20
Belshazzar	Daniel 5:23
Babylonians	Habakkuk 1:7, 11
Simon the sorcerer	Acts 8:9
Herod	Acts 12:20-23

What does the Bible state about people who are self-exalting?

Psalm 18:27 – "For thou wilt save the afflicted people; but wilt bring down high looks" (KJV; also the following two).

Isaiah 2:11 – "The lofty looks of man shall be humbled, and the haughtiness of men shall be bowed down, and the Lord alone shall be exalted in that day."

Isaiah 10:12 – "I will punish the fruit of the stout heart of the king of Assyria, and the glory of his high looks." High looks is defined as proud attitude.

Pride and self-exaltation are not just found in Biblical characters. In 1 Corinthians 10:12 Paul warns, "So, if you think you are standing firm, be careful that you don't fall." In our society, many people who appear to be standing tall with esteem and success have come crashing down. Dwight Gooden, a former pitcher for the New York Mets, is a good example of this. He has been out of baseball for 16 months as a result of a 60-day drug suspension that started June 28, 1994. This suspension on November 4, 1994 was increased to cover the whole 1995 season. He was National League "Rookie of the Year" in 1984 and received the Cy Young award for the best pitcher in the National League in 1985. He led the national league in strikeouts (268) and had 24 victories that year. He had surgery on his rotator cuff in 1991. This was the last year that he had more wins than losses.

In a *People* magazine interview Gooden was talking about his success. He said, "I think it's just a God-given talent. Plus, when you get in tough situations, like the bases loaded and nobody out, you never give in. Just keep feeling like you're the best out there. You got the ball in your hands and you're in command . . . ."[1] Gooden was later arrested for drug possession and is out of baseball.

In *Life* magazine John DeLorean was quoted as saying, "I was a pretty sick and strange guy. I was arrogant beyond belief, so arrogant, I believed I had humility."[2]

Those Whose Esteem Was Too Low

There are several people in the Bible who had low self-esteem. The first two people in Bible to have low esteem were *Adam* and *Eve*. This is why they wanted to be like God (Gen. 3). The first story in the Bible deals with low self-esteem. It is about the creation of mankind and the world. There were four people in the garden who were perfect, without sin at one time. They were God, Satan (he started out perfect), Adam, and Eve. Only two realized it; God and Satan. Low self-esteem seems to be one of the factors that prompted Adam and Eve to fall into Satan's temptation.

Several others have had low esteem as well:

Moses had low self-esteem. One of the reasons he did not want to speak to Pharaoh was because he did not believe in himself. His three excuses back up this idea. In Exodus 3:11 Moses said to God, "Who am I, that I should go to Pharaoh and bring the Israelites out of Egypt?" In Exodus 4:1 Moses said to God, "What if they do not believe me or listen to me . . . ?" In verse 11 Moses insults himself by saying, "I have never been eloquent, neither in the past nor since you have spoken to your servant. I am slow of speech and tongue." This was not true. Stephen said in Acts 7:22, "Moses was educated in all the wisdom of the Egyptians and was powerful in speech and action."

King Saul had low self-esteem because he was jealous of David for killing Goliath. First Samuel 18:8-9 states, "Saul was very angry; this refrain galled him. 'They have credited David with (killing) tens of thousands,' he thought, 'but me with only thousands. What more can he get but the kingdom?' And from that time on Saul kept a jealous eye on David."

Joseph's brothers had low esteem because they were jealous of Joseph. Stephen said of Joseph's brothers in Acts 7:9, "Because the patriarchs were jealous of Joseph, they sold him as a slave into Egypt. But God was with him."

Rachel had low esteem because she was jealous that Leah had children with Jacob and she did not. "When Rachel saw that she was not bearing Jacob any children, she became jealous of her sister and said to Jacob, 'Give me children, or I'll die'!" (Gen. 30:1).

Leah had low esteem. This was due partly to the fact that she knew Jacob loved Rachel, her younger sister, more. Genesis 29:30 — ". . . he (Jacob) loved Rachel more than Leah." The description of Leah is enough to give anyone a "complex." She is described as having weak eyes but Rachel was described as lovely in form and beauty (Gen. 29:17).

Some Jews had low self-esteem because they were jealous of Paul and Silas. "But the Jews were jealous; so they rounded up some bad characters from the marketplace, formed a mob and started a riot in the city. They rushed to Jason's house in search of Paul and Silas in order to bring them out to the crowd" (Acts 17:5).

Some other Jews had low self-esteem because they were jealous of Paul because of the crowd size he had around him when he taught. "When the Jews saw the crowds, they were filled with jealousy and talked abusively against what Paul was saying" (Acts 13:45).

The high priest and Sadducees had low self-esteem after being around the apostles. "Then the high priest and all his associates, who were members of the Sadducees, were filled with jealousy. They arrested the apostles and put them in the public jail" (Acts 5:17-18).

Those Who Had Good Self-Esteem

Some people who had a good biblical, God-centered esteem:

David (1 Sam. 17:14-57). David is probably the person with the best God-centered self-esteem of all those mentioned in the Bible. It was a great asset to him being King and a conquering hero.

What question did David ask about the man who kills Goliath (17:26)? What does he get? David wanted to know this before he killed Goliath. He wanted to see if it was worth it. Do you think he went and "checked out" the King's daughter? Most definitely.

How did Eliab his oldest brother describe David (17:28)? Eliab insulted him by calling him "only a shepherd." He also told David that he was conceited and had a wicked heart. How many men in the armies actually believed David could kill Goliath? Only one. David was the only one who believed he could do it. All the other men were betting on Goliath! Eliab wrongly interpreted David's Godly self-esteem as conceit and wickedness. Our world does the same thing today. People with a good self-esteem are often labeled as conceited. Rush Limbaugh comes to mind. I do not believe he is conceited, but he is definitely bold in his beliefs. This could be one of the reasons many people don't like him.

Why do you think David picked up five smooth stones (17:40)? It was actually because David knew that Goliath had other brothers and he did not want to be defenseless. Goliath had at least one brother whose name was Lahmi (1 Chron. 20:5). It was not because he was afraid he would miss Goliath. David thought Goliath was too big to miss, while the others thought he was too big to kill. David also thought he might have to kill some other men. He would need something which with to attack them. Four stones was enough to make him undefeatable, because with God four stones can defeat a nation.

What did David do when he met Goliath (17:46)? He told him he was going to kill him and cut off his head. How did he do this? With Goliath's own sword! He was extremely bold and cocky. Who did David say was with him (17:47)? The Lord. David was the first person who did what to Goliath? He was the first person who stood up to Goliath's challenge and won. What did David do with the head after he killed Goliath (17:51, 54, 57)? He took it to Jerusalem and showed it off.

How did David's esteem get out of hand (2 Sam. 11:1-5)? When he had the affair with Bathsheba his esteem had gotten out of hand. He knew that he was the King and could have anything he wanted, even if what he wanted was another man's wife. One of the ironies about this story is that the husband of Bathsheba (Uriah) was one of David's "mighty men" (1 Chron. 11:41). David knew this man intimately.

Shadrach, Meshach and Abednego (Dan. 3:16-23). Why didn't these three guys give in to the heat of the furnace or King Nebuchadnezzar? Because they believed God would take care of them. Previously, I mentioned that I thought King Nebuchadnezzar had too high self-esteem. This might have been one of the reasons he was so hostile when Shadrach, Meshach and Abednego did not go along with what he wanted.

Noah (Gen. 6:9-16). What do you think Noah went through in building the ark? He had to face a lot of criticism from his neighbors. He was the only one in his subdivision who was building an ark.

Daniel (Dan. 6:3-16; 9:23; 10:11). Why did these men tell on Daniel? They did not like Daniel. What was their problem with him? They were jealous of him.

Joshua (Josh. 5:13-6:27). How do you know Joshua had courage and good self-esteem? Because he convinced the people of Israel to go along with God's battle plan.

Gideon (Judg. 7:1-25). How do you think Gideon felt about losing all those men for the upcoming battle? He had to feel bad about this because a general is going to want as many men as he could get. Gideon had faith in God and convinced the soldiers to fight God's way.

Paul (1 Cor. 4:3-4; Acts 20:26). How could Paul not condemn himself for his past behavior? Because he knew that God forgave him.

Job (Job 12:3; 13:2). What did Job's three friends continually do to him after his losses? They constantly blamed him for the losses. One of the frequent causes of the feeling of inferiority is people carefully watching us to see if we mess up (Luke 14:1-2).

> There is no such thing as a "superiority complex." There is self-centeredness or self will. But what appears to be superior attitudes are likely to be a cover for inadequate feelings. It is common knowledge, verified by clinicians and therapists in mental hygiene, that we rate ourselves too low. Why? Partially because of disappointments and frustrations encountered in growing up. Many of us have been ridiculed, humiliated, berated somewhere along the line.[3]

Joseph (Gen. 39:13-23). To whom was Joseph committed? God.

John the Baptist (Mark 6:14-20). Did John know his advice would cost him his head? Yes, but he was bold enough to state the truth anyway.

Did you notice the difference between those with an inappropriaet self-esteem, and those who had a God-centered esteem? By understanding who we are in God's eyes, we can correct our esteem. Let's look at how much God knows about us, and why he loves us.

Notes

1. *People*, December 23, 1985, p. 77.

2. *Life*, January 1986.

3. William R. Parker and Elaine St. John, *Prayer Can Change Your Life* (Carmel, NY: Guidepost), p.73.

8 Who Are We Actually?

This is probably the most important question in building a healthy esteem. Charles Swindoll wrote, "You are, before the Lord, a very important person. This is not just good psychology; this is good, sound Biblical doctrine."

James Mallory wrote,

At this point we are once again confronted with the relevance of Christianity to mental health. As we said, the person who has problems with his self-image and feels of little worth anticipates rejection, tries to impress, becomes hostile, or behaves in other distinctive ways. But the person who has really and truly found Jesus Christ can answer this identity question in a positive manner. "I am a joint heir with Jesus Christ. I am a son of God. I am tremendously important in the sight of God. Christ died for me, and I am acceptable to him. He is living within me. We have a union, a relationship. There are also values, principles, ethics, that I can count on. I can follow them. They work."[1]

God Describes Us

There are two "S's" that God would use to describe us.

1. *Splendor* (Isa. 55:5; 60:9). This word is defined as great

brightness and luster; brilliance; magnificent richness and glory. Psalm 8:4-5 states, "What is man that you are mindful of him, the son of man that you care for him? You made him a little lower than the heavenly beings and crowned him with glory and honor."

2. *Sacred* (1 Cor. 3:16-17; 6:19) comes from the Latin word for "holy." The Greek word for "sacred" means the same thing.

Jesus speaks of our value according to God:

Matthew 6:26 — "Are you not much more valuable than they (birds)?"

Matthew 12:12 — "How much more valuable is a man than a sheep!"

Luke 12:24 — "And how much more valuable you are than birds!"

There are two parables that Jesus told about the value that God has for man. In Luke 15 Jesus tells the parables about the lost sheep and the lost coin. In the lost sheep Jesus told about a man who had 100 sheep. Ninety-nine of them were safe and accounted for. One of them was lost. This man cared so much about the lost one that he left the 99 and went looking for the one that was lost. He searched until he found it. When he found it, he laid it on his shoulders and took it back home (Luke 15:7).

In the parable of the lost coin, a woman had 10 silver coins. She lost one of them. She cared so much about the lost one that she called her friends to come and help her find it. When she found it her friends rejoiced with her (Luke 15:8-10). These two parables teach that Jesus and God want us in heaven probably more than we want to be there!

Many Christians have no idea of who they are or how valuable they are in the eyes of God. They have never made Calvary a personal experience. Isaiah 17:7 shows us where a person can get a view of their value, "In that day men will look to their Maker and turn their eyes to the Holy One of Israel." It is from their Maker that a person gains their esteem.

Even the government of the United States has no idea who Christians are. If the government knew who Christians were they would give us all *green cards* (Phil. 3:20; Eph. 2:19; 1 Pet. 2:11). The United States government gives aliens in the United States green cards so that they can work and live here. Different translations of the above verses give different titles for who Christians are. According to these verses Christians are aliens, pilgrims and strangers in a foreign land.

I would recommend that when you are teaching this lesson that you give all of the participants green pieces of cardboard that they can keep in their billfold or purse. On these "green cards" put three verses: Philippians 3:20; Ephesians 2:19; 1 Peter 2:11. I keep one of these cards in my billfold all the time to remind me who I am because the world is continually telling me who I am not. This green card is a good visual lesson to help Christians remember that they are aliens in this world.

It is important that we understand what we are without Christ. In Genesis 6:5 it states that man before the flood was wicked, and his heart was evil all the time. Things probably aren't much different now. Genesis 8:21 teaches that man is evil from childhood.

God Values Us

The Bible also teaches that God values man. First Corinthians 6:20 states, "You were bought at a price. Therefore honor God with your body." How valuable are you in the sight of God according to Mark 5:11-13? Jesus paid 2000 pigs for the ransom of one man's soul. What would 2000 pigs be worth in today's money? Approximately $250,000.00. This is nowhere near how valuable we are to God. He gave all he had to ransom mankind from hell.

According to Isaiah 66:2 what three things does God esteem in man? (The Hebrew word for esteem means to "lift up my eyes to.")
1. a humble spirit
2. a contrite spirit
3. a person who trembles at the word of God

How well does God know his creation? Charles L. Allen wrote,

"He knows we have groceries to buy, rent or payments to make on our houses, clothes that are necessary, expenses of the children in school, bills of every sort to meet. Not only that, he knows we have desires and wants beyond our bare necessities." The Bible teaches several concepts about God knowing or noticing us:

God knows every hair on our head (Matt. 10:30).

God knew us before we were born (Jer. 1:5).

God knows us by name (Exod. 33:17).

God knows us personally (John 10:14, 27).

Whom did Jesus notice and value? There are many people, but Luke 8:40-48 and Luke 19:1-7 give my two favorite ones that Jesus valued. In Luke 8:40-48 it is the woman who had been sick for 12 years. Jesus did not have to heal her, but he showed her he valued her when he did. In Luke 19:1-7 it is Zacchaeus. He could have made fun of Zacchaeus up in the tree, but he never did. I am sure Zacchaeus was surprised Jesus noticed him and wanted to spend time with him. How was Zacchaeus' esteem before he met Jesus? It must have been low because he worked for the Roman government, was very wealthy and was short. How was his esteem after he met Jesus? It totally changed and produced repentance in his life.

Jesus taught that what man values is detestable to God (Luke 16:15). In this verse, Jesus is talking about money. This is one of the things that man values. Man also values the outside appearance (1 Sam. 16:7) as well. God values and looks at the heart of a man, not his appearance. First Peter 3:3-4 teaches that a person's beauty should come from the inside.

Who are we in God's eyes? The truest picture of who we are is found in Scripture!

One of Satan's goals is to prevent people from knowing who they really are, and how valuable they are! This is one of the ways he can kill, steal, and destroy people (John 10:10). Psalm 8 gives us a clear indication of how valuable we are. This psalm is one that talks about the dignity of man. It proclaims,

"Oh Lord, our Lord,

how majestic is your name in all the earth!

142

You have set your glory
    above the heavens.
From the lips of children and infants
    you have ordained praise
because of your enemies,
    to silence the foe and the avenger.
When I consider your heavens,
    the works of your fingers,
the moon and the stars,
    which you have set in place,
What is man that you are mindful of him,
    the son of man that you care for him?
You made him a little lower than the heavenly beings
    and crowned him with glory and honor.
You made him ruler over the works of your hands;
    you put everything under his feet;
all flocks and herds,
    and the beasts of the field,
the birds of the air,
    and the fish of the sea,
    all that swim the paths of the seas.
O Lord, our Lord,
    how majestic is your name in all the earth!

When read in conjunction with Genesis 1:26-27 which says, "Then God said, 'Let us make man in our image, in our likeness, and let them rule over the fish of the sea and the birds of the air, over the livestock, over all the earth, and over all the creatures that move along the ground.' So God created man in his own image, in the image of God he created him; male and female he created them," we see that man was created in God's image. David wrote in Psalm 139:14 about man's creation when he wrote, "I praise you because I am fearfully and wonderfully made; your works are wonderful, I know that full well." Isaiah also wrote about man's creation. It states in Isaiah 43:1, "But now, this is what the Lord says – he who created you, O Jacob, he who formed you, O Israel: 'Fear not, for I have redeemed you; I have called you by name; you are mine'." Isaiah 44:2 proclaims, "This is what the Lord says — he who made you, who formed you in the womb, and who will help you: Do not be afraid, O Jacob, my servant, Jeshurun, whom I have chosen."

When a person looks at God's creation, he is seeing the personality of God. The more a person learns about God, the more the person learns about himself. Elizabeth O'Connor wrote, "Knowing oneself and knowing God are not two separate things. They are a seamless robe, one intricately bound to the other."[2]

It is easy to understand then that our self-esteem should be anchored in our creator and the value our Creator places on us. God created man a little lower than the angels and God, and has crowned man with glory and honor (Psa. 8:5). Mankind tends to forget where he is on the creation scale. One of the reasons for this is because it is very difficult for man to actually see himself the way God sees him.

Why should the Bible be the ultimate source of self-esteem? The Bible is the "Blue book" for humanity. It is the book that tells us who we are and what our value is to God. It is the book that tells of our creation and God's crucifixion to redeem his creation. All people need to read, understand and follow their care instructions which come from the Bible.

As we end this chapter it is important to look at Jesus' life and death to gain a clearer indication of our value to God. The next chapter will discuss the greatest esteem-causing event in history: Calvary.

Notes

1. James D. Mallory, *The Kink and I* (Grand Rapids: Zondervan, 1973), pp. 109-110.

2. Elizabeth O'Connor, *Cry Pain, Cry Hope.*

9 Calvary as the Proof of Our Value to God

What took place at Calvary is the greatest event in the history of the world! It is the event and place where God shouted how much he loved man. It shows how much he was willing to pay to redeem man from Hell. It is the place where man can figure out his worth to God. Calvary is the greatest compliment that God ever paid man — that he thought enough of mankind that he would die for his fallen, sinful creation to give us a new chance for a new birth. The death of Jesus is mentioned over 170 times directly in the New Testament. It is the foundation of Christianity. It is also the foundation of a person's self-esteem!

David A. Fiensy wrote about crucifixion, "Crucifixion was considered the worst form of execution in antiquity, even worse than execution by burning or by wild animals. Origen, the third century theologian, who was probably in a position to have witnessed a crucifixion, called it 'the utterly vile death.'"[1]

Personal Worth

Peter addressed Calvary and man's value. In 1 Peter 1:18-19 he wrote, "For you know that it was not with perishable things such as silver or gold that you were redeemed from the empty way of life handed down to you from your forefathers, but with the precious blood of Christ, a lamb without blemish or defect." We mean so much to God that he was willing to sacrifice his beloved Son, to suffer in our place, to restore us to fellowship with him (John 3:16). Paul wrote about the cross, "May I never boast except in the cross of our Lord Jesus Christ, through which the world has been crucified to me, and I to the world" (Gal. 6:14). Why would one boast about the cross?

The answer may be in the question, "What am I worth as a person?" I'm not talking about the value of the chemicals contained within your physical body, but you as a whole. What could possibly be used as the standard of measure to come up with the answer? I believe that Josh McDowell had the answer when he wrote, "A healthy self-image is being committed to the truth of God's estimation of you."[2] He is exactly right. The standard of a man's esteem comes from God's value of us! For a person's esteem to be consistent, there needs to be a consistent measurement that can be used to assess the value of mankind. That consistent measurement comes from a hill that had three crosses on it.

John DeVines, author of *How Much Are You Worth?*, writes:

The answer to how much I am worth determines
whether I am happy or sad,
excited or depressed,
in love with life
or thinking about suicide.

If I think that I am valuable — worth a lot —
I will function well at my job,
get along better with my spouse,
and have a tremendous sense of well-being.
But if I think I am worthless,
I lack motivation for work,
and am convinced that everything I do will fail.[3]

Paul wrote a lot about how much we are worth to God. He writes in Ephesians 5:2, ". . . and live a life of love, just as Christ loved us and gave himself up for us as a fragrant offering and sacrifice to God." Paul wrote to Titus in Titus 2:13-14, ". . . while we wait for the blessed hope — the glorious appearing of our great God and Savior, Jesus Christ, who gave himself for us to redeem us from all wickedness and to purify for himself a people that are his very own, eager to do what is good." In both of these verses Paul mentions the idea that Christ gave himself for us. The reason for this sacrifice is found in the Old Testament law. The writer of Hebrews tells about this law in 9:22, "In fact, the law requires that nearly everything be cleansed with blood, and without the shedding of blood there is no forgiveness." Jesus died so that we could be forgiven by God and could go to heaven. This death shows how much Christ and God care for and love us! Calvary should be the foundation of a biblical self-esteem.

Importance of Biblical Self-Esteem

Why is a good biblical self-esteem so important? Your esteem affects every area of your life. Good esteem is a predictor of success in almost every area of life. Zig Ziglar sees self-image as the first step to success.[4] Research back in the early '60s showed the effect that other people's opinions have on self-esteem and success. Payne and Farquhar found evidence suggesting that a negative "mirror self-concept" goes with underachievement; that is, the child who believes that others think ill of him, and thinks ill of himself, reflects this poor opinion in his school achievement.[5] As stated before — success begins with a good self-esteem. I frequently give people this "Formula For Success":

$$S = GG + CBE + APCO - F$$

Success (S) — The favorable or desired outcome of a task.

Godly Goals (GG) — Having specific plans to attain a goal that praises God. My favorite verse on goals in the Bible is 2 Corinthians

5:9 which says, "So we make it our goal to please him, whether we are at home in the body or away from it." This is the primary goal of all Christians!

Correct Biblical Esteem (CBE) — Knowing who you are biblically in the image of God.

Appropriate Plans Carried Out (APCO) — Carrying out adequate plans to get the task accomplished.

Fear (F) — fear.

If the above equation is correct, then correct biblical esteem is a vital ingredient to being successful. From my perspective, it is the main ingredient. John Vasconcellos, a state Assemblyman from California, sponsored a bill that created *California's Task Force to Promote Self-Esteem and Personal and Social Responsibility* in 1987. He said, "Self-esteem precedes doing."

As stated previously, our esteem should come from our Creator and Savior. Blaise Pascal said, "Apart from Christ we know neither what our life or death is; we do not know what God is nor what we ourselves are." It should be from our Creator that we learn about ourselves (Matt. 11:29). What does this mean for non-Christians? This means that non-Christians know very little about themselves and have absolutely no stable basis for their self-esteem. I will say it again, it is important that you learn to build your esteem on **Calvary**. Calvary declares God's value for man. The ringing of the hammer against the nails tells man how valuable he is to God. It is important that we remember who Jesus is if we are going to have good biblical self-esteem! (Exod. 3:14).

Plastic is found in a lot of products used in American households. It is used in furniture and in soda bottles. It has become a strong substance and has replaced much of the metal in automobiles. It has definitely made our lives easier and better. One Sunday during the Christmas season, the minister's message was on the past life of Jesus. He talked about who Jesus was before he became Immanuel in Bethlehem. As he spoke, my eyes focused under the communion table. What I found was a plastic baby Jesus. A plastic Prince of Peace. I have also seen a concrete statue of Jesus. What a strange concept, a cement Savior! Both the plastic and cement Savior cannot feel. They are both cold and uncaring.

Jesus' Identity

But we know that Jesus does feel. He can fully understand everything we have been through. Hebrews 4:15 states, "For we do not have a high priest who is unable to sympathize with our weaknesses, but we have one who has been tempted in every way, just as we are — yet was without sin." But until we know who he was and why he died for us, he is cement and plastic to us.

Who was this Jesus who died at Calvary? Jesus is King (Matt. 27:11; John 18:37). Jesus is Prince and Savior (Acts 5:31). Jesus is the bread of life, those who come to him will never be hungry (John 6:35). He is the light of the world (John 8:12). He is from above (John 8:23). He is the Son of God. He was glorified by God. He is not a liar (John 8:54-55). He is the good shepherd who knows his sheep (us) and we know him (John 10:11). He and God are one (John 10:30). He is the resurrection and the life. People who believe in him will never die (John 11:25-26). He is our Teacher and Lord (John 13:13). Jesus is a Wonderful Counselor, Mighty God, Everlasting Father, Prince of Peace (Isa. 9:6).

It is important to build your esteem on the last week of Jesus' life! Jesus knew what was going to happen to him (Luke 18:31-33). What does this tell us about Jesus? This should tell us that we are very important to God. Jesus **chose** to die for us. He was not forced by God to die (John 10:18; Matt. 26:53-54). Romans 5:6 states, "You see, at just the right time, when we were still powerless, Christ died for the ungodly. Very rarely will anyone die for a righteous man, though for a good man someone might dare to die. But God demonstrates his own love for us in this: While we were still sinners, Christ died for us" (Compare John 3:16.) It is this great choice that should give Christians a good, healthy self-esteem. Let's look at the last three days of Jesus's life.

Friday

Often referred to as Good Friday — is a day from which Christians can gain their self-esteem. Let's look at the events that lead up to the death of Jesus. Through them we will find out how much value Jesus places on us.

Jesus' Trial before the Sanhedrin (Matt. 26:62-68)

☦ Accused of blasphemy
☦ Abused by the Sanhedrin
  † They spit in his face.
  † They slapped him.
  † They struck him with their fists.

Jesus before Pilate (Matt. 27:11-26)

☦ Barabbas was released and Jesus was sentenced to death.
☦ Jesus was whipped with a whip that had nine tails. Each of these tails contained rock, lead, and glass. As it was drawn across the back, all the skin would be removed. From the bottom of the base of his head to the soles of his feet, Jesus' back had no flesh. He was a bloodied mess. "His blood was for you."

Jesus Abused by a Company of Soldiers (Matt. 27:27-31)

☦ They stripped him and put a scarlet robe on him.
☦ They put a crown of thorns on his head. The facial cuts that Jesus sustained would have bled profusely. Jesus was a bloody mess.
☦ They mocked him saying "Hail King of the Jews."
☦ They spit on him.
☦ They struck him on the head while he wore the crown of thorns.
☦ They repeatedly put a robe on and off him, reopening the wounds.
☦ They led him away to crucify him.

Jesus' Crucifixion (Matt. 27:35, 39-44)

Square, flat nails were driven between the small bones on both wrists and then into the cross. This would paralyze the chest muscles making it almost impossible to exhale. A square, flat nail was pounded in the middle of both feet and then into the cross.

Jesus' Death (Matt. 27:50-53)

A person who dies from crucifixion dies because of exposure and a broken heart. The heart was squeezed by the lungs because they could not exhale. This was a very painful way to die. This is probably the most painful way to die known to man. The Supreme court would not allow this kind of execution today because it would be classified as cruel *and* unusual!

David A. Fiensy wrote, "The medical causes of his death are usually given as shock and exhaustion due to blood loss and inability to breathe freely while hanging on the cross."[6]

If you were Christ, would you have died for a person like yourself? Would you have chosen to die this way? Jesus had to see tremendous value and worth in us to die for us, let alone to die in the way that he did. It is important that you meet Christ on the road carrying his cross and you ask him why he is doing this (Heb. 10:10). He is doing this for us so that we can go to heaven. He was the only sacrifice that would allow us to go to heaven (John 14:6). What other questions would you like to ask Jesus about his value for you as he is carrying the cross on the road to Calvary?

Now that we have learned of our importance to God, what do we do to mend our broken esteem? In the next chapter we will discuss the spiritual surgery we need to perform in order to correct faulty esteem in ourselves, or in others.

Notes

1. David A. Fiensy, *New Testament Introduction* (Joplin, MO: College Press, 1994), p. 113.

2. Josh McDowell, *His Image . . . My Image* (San Bernardino, CA: Here's Life Publishers, Inc., 1984), p. 98.

3. John DeVines, *How Much Are You Worth?* (Grand Rapids: Bibles for India), pp. 3-4.

4. Zig Ziglar, *See You at the Top* (Gretna, LA: Pelican Publishing Co., 1983).

5. D.E. Payne and W. Farquhar, "The dimensions of an objective measure of academic self-concept," *Journal of Educational Psychology*, 53 (1962), pp. 187-192.

6. David A Fiensy, *New Testament Introduction*, p. 115.

10 Ways to Build Esteem in Yourself and Others

If a person really wants to improve their self-esteem they should take more time doing surgery on the eternal spiritual side of themselves. This type of surgery is what David prayed about in Psalm 139:1, 23-24, "O Lord, you have searched me and you know me. Search me, O God and know my heart; test me and know my anxious thoughts. See if there is any offensive way in me, and lead me in the way everlasting." Being found pure and unoffensive in the sight of God should do wonders for a person's self-esteem. There are several things a person can do to improve his or her esteem.

Pray for the Three R's

One of the first things a person can do to improve his or her self-esteem is to pray. There are three things that should be prayed for: *renewal*, *revival* and *restoration* of the soul and spirit. These three R's can have a great impact on the self and self-esteem.

Isaiah 40:31 assures that God renews strength. David wrote several Psalms about these three traits. David understood that the law of the Lord revives the soul (Psa. 19:7). He understood that God restored his soul (Psa. 23:3; 51:12). David understood that renewal of his spirit came from God (Psa. 51:10).

The words "soul" and "spirit" appear in all of these verses. This is because low esteem is a crushed spirit and soul. David knew what it was like to have a crushed spirit (Psa. 34:18; 38:8). David knew what needed to be done to the spirit and he knew who could do it. It is the renewal, revival, and restoration of the spirit and soul that will improve self-esteem.

Develop the Five C's

It is also important that a person with low esteem seek the development of the five C's of a healthy self-esteem. These C's are traits of the Spirit of God that he wants to develop within Christians. These C's are by-products of Christianity. They are invaluable tools in life. They set and direct the course of life. Every one of these traits was possessed by people God has used in mighty ways. The C's are:

Courage

"Courage" comes from the Latin word *cor* and the French word *courage*, both meaning "heart" or "spirit." The word courage in Greek is *tharsos* meaning "to be of good cheer." It is also from the Greek word *tharreo* meaning "to be of good courage; bold." This word is found in 2 Corinthians 5:6, 8; 7:16; 10:1, 2; Hebrews 13:6.

Courage is an attitude of facing or dealing with anything recognized as dangerous, difficult or painful, instead of withdrawing from it. It is being brave, and having valor. Sydney Smith said, "A great deal of talent is lost to the world for want of a little courage." A little courage, like a little faith, can move mountains. The Bible teaches that courage can:

      fail – Joshua 2:11

      be no longer had – Joshua 5:1

      be lost – 2 Samuel 4:1

be found – 2 Samuel 7:27; 1 Chronicles 17:25
be taken – 2 Chronicles 15:8; Ezra 10:4; Mark 6:50
act – 2 Chronicles 19:11
melt away – Psalm 107:26
endure – Ezekiel 22:14
been seen – Acts 4:13
be taken – Acts 23:11
be ours in Christ – 2 Corinthians 3:4
be kept – Acts 27:22, 25
be sufficient – Philippians 1:20
be held onto – Hebrews 3:6
be part of us because of God's hand – Ezra 7:28

Courage is a building block for esteem because it is what causes people to be persistent (to stand firm and keep on trying) even when they are afraid. Hebrews 10:36; 12:1 reminds us that we need to persevere to receive what God has promised. Jesus said in Luke 21:19, "By standing firm you gain life." Jesus spoke of perseverance in Matthew 10:22, "All men will hate you because of me, but he who stands firm to the end will be saved." Perseverence is possible only with courage!

Babe Ruth showed that perseverance produces results. Without it he would never have accomplished what he did. He said, "I just keep goin' up there and swingin' at 'em." He was at one time the record holder for most home runs in a career in major league baseball. He is also the record holder for striking out the most in a career. He is remembered for his hits and not his misses.

Confidence

This comes from the Latin word *confidentia*. It is from the root words *fides* meaning "belief," and *federe*, "to trust, to have faith." Confidence is the fact of being certain or assured. It is the belief in one's abilities. Confidence in self is dangerous (Luke 18:9; Phil. 3:1-11). The Bible teaches that confidence:

can be seen by others; it can be questioned – 2 Kings 18:19
is gained by knowing God is with us – 2 Chronicles 32:8

can be found in hard times — Psalm 27:1-3, 13
is found through God — Psalm 71:5; Proverbs 3:26
is a result of righteousness — Isaiah 32:17
is in God — Jeremiah 17:7
can be found in our speech — Acts 2:29
helps us to approach God boldly — Ephesians 3:12; Hebrews 4:16
is in the Lord — Philippians 2:24; 2 Thessalonians 3:4
should not be in our flesh — Philippians 3:3-4
is in God — Hebrews 13:6
can be thrown away — Hebrews 10:35

It is confidence in God that boosts esteem!

Competence

Comes from the Latin word *compententia*. Competence means meeting agreement, sufficient for the need. The Bible teaches that Christians are competent:
to instruct — Romans 15:14
to make judgment over trivial matters — 1 Corinthians 6:2
through God, not ourselves — 2 Corinthians 3:5

Competence is important for esteem because it helps us to deal with the challenges people will throw at us.

Commitment

Comes from the Latin word *committere*. It means to bring together a mission, a pledge or promise to do something. The Bible teaches about commitment:
hearts must be fully committed to God — 1 Kings 8:61; 15:14
heart fully committed to God — 2 Chronicles 15:17; 16:9; 34:16
we should commit our ministries to God — Acts 14:23

Our commitment to Christ is what allows God to strengthen us!

Completeness

Comes from the Latin word *completus*. It means to fill up.

Lacking no component or part, full, entire, accomplished, skilled, successfully executed. The completeness teachings in the Bible are:

work can be completed by the grace of God – Acts 14:26

complete in knowledge through God – Romans 15:14

Completeness allows us to be prepared and equip us for every good work (2 Tim. 3:17).

Prescription to Improve Your Self-Esteem

To improve your self-esteem in other ways try doing the following.

☞ Spend time with God, reading the Bible (2 Tim. 3:16-17). Ask him to teach you who you are (Matt. 11:29; Luke 10:40-42; Isa. 54:13). Joshua 1:8 tells us to read our Bibles day and night. It urges, "Do not let this book of the law depart from your mouth; meditate on it day and night, so that you may be careful to do everything written in it. Then you will be prosperous and successful." Bruce Parmenter wrote, "Worship is a great antidote to low self-esteem."[1] It is from daily Bible study and worship that the Lord will teach us what is right, and direct our ways (Isa. 48:17). This is what Mary chose to do and she was blessed because of it (Luke 10:38-42). She chose to sit at Jesus' feet and listen to what he had to say. We all need to learn to do this!

You may ask, "but what do I need to learn from the Lord?" I can think of at least four things:

❖ Who you are.

❖ How valuable you are.

❖ Who is always with you.

❖ What you should be doing with your life.

One of the best chapters in the Bible to read to improve your self-esteem is Psalm 139. This psalm has many great promises that tell about God and his knowledge of us. Verses 1-6 are promises that God knows us intimately. Verses 7-12 are promises that God will always be with us. Verses 13-16 are promises that God knew us before our birth. This idea relates to Jeremiah 1:5 which states, "Before I formed you in the womb I knew you, before you were born I set you apart; I appointed you as a prophet to the nations." Ephesians 1:4 states, "For he chose us in him before the creation of the world to be holy and blameless in his sight."

☞ Remember your successes. Remember that your life has purpose and that God will not abandon you. Work from your point(s) of strength (1 Sam. 18:14-15; Psa. 138:8).

☞ Stop dwelling on the past failures. Learn from your past failures. Keep trying to succeed (Isa. 43:18).

☞ State positives about yourself. Watch out for your negative internal communication (Phil. 4:8).

☞ Make it a goal to learn the true value of yourself in God's eyes (John 3:16-17; 10:18; Matt. 26:53-54).

☞ Learn to say thank you to praise. Stop rolling your eyes to compliments. Stop blowing off compliments. Learn to take them as a child would! (1 Thess. 5:18; Matt. 18:3).

☞ Have realistic expectations of yourself with God's help (Matt. 14:25-31).

☞ Do a weekly inventory of positive traits you see in yourself (1 Tim. 4:4). There have to be good things about you because God believes you are worth redeeming. David understood how valuable he was to God. My paraphrase of what David wrote in Psalm 139:6 is "I know how valuable I am to you and this just blows my mind."

☞ Watch out for the negative, critical people with whom you associate (Prov. 12:26; 22:24-25; 1 Cor. 15:33).

☞ Set goals for yourself that can be reached with reasonable effort (Prov. 29:18, KJV). Alfred Adler said, "We cannot think, feel, will or act without the perception of some goal."[2] Henry David Thoreau said, "If one advances confidently in the direction of his dreams, and endeavors to live the life which he has imagined, he will be met with a success unexpected in common hours."[3]

☞ Get out of the blue jeans and sweats when you can. Dress up when you can (Esth. 2:3, 9). It is perfectly all right to want to look your best.

☞ Smile and maintain good eye contact (Mark 3:5).

☞ Try new things. Take some risks. Peter took the risk to walk on the water (Matt. 14:27-29). Maxwell Maltz said, "We must have courage to bet on our ideas, to take the calculated risk, and to act. Everyday living requires courage if life is to be effective and bring happiness."

☞ Become your best friend. Treat yourself the way you treat other people. Be compassionate to yourself (Col. 3:12).

☞ Learn to value the things in yourself that are valuable to God (Luke 16:15).

☞ Stop wanting to be someone you are never going to be, and probably should not be. Accept yourself for who you are (Rom. 15:7). In August of 1995, *Family Circle* and *Young Miss* did a survey with 45,000 teenage girls and their mothers. Thirty-five percent of the teenage girls want to be like supermodel Cindy Crawford when they grow up.[3] Kaz Cooke, the author of *Real Gorgeous: The Truth about Body and Beauty*, quotes Cindy Crawford as saying, "I think women see me on the cover of magazines and think I never have a pimple or bags under my eyes. You have to realize that's after two hours of hair and makeup, plus [photo] retouching. Even I don't wake up looking like Cindy Crawford."[4]

☞ Become assertive with your opinions and beliefs. People will respect you more for doing this. You don't have to push your ideas down people's throats, but you can state them gently yet firmly.

☞ If a person defends himself from criticism or disrespectful behaviors this a good way to build self-esteem. This is exactly what Jesus did when he faced criticism. He was accused of being the devil repeatedly. His paraphrased response was "Prove it" (John 8:46). Frequently the reason a person does not defend him/herself is because he or she doesn't want to hurt the other person's feelings. The only problem with this is that they end up hurting and disrespecting themselves and lowering their self-esteem.

Building Self-Esteem in Others

Here are 13 biblical ways to accomplish this goal! Before building a person's esteem it is important to gain an understanding of why it is low. This means you have to know them for who they are and what they have been through before you can build their esteem. Approval and support are greatly needed to build their esteem. People need a shoulder more than a scolder.

1. Allow them to state their opinions. If they have a hard time doing this, encourage them to tell you how they feel. Let them know that they will not be rejected for what they say (Matt. 16:13-20).

2. Let them realize it is OK to disagree and there will not be criticism, rejection or isolation if a disagreement occurs (Acts 15:36-40).

3. Teach them to think for themselves and make their own decisions. Don't pamper and rescue them (Prov. 19:19, 29:21). When people face problems and solve them this builds esteem and confidence. It is good to help teach them skills that can build their esteem. Be their coach and cheerleader, not just their coach.

4. Teach them to acknowledge and use their gifts and see themselves as useful (1 Pet. 4:10). The best way to do this is to praise and encourage them (Eph. 4:29). Also be kind and compassionate to them (Eph. 4:32). Achievements are great esteem builders.

5. Allow them to express anger in healthy ways. You may have to teach them how to do this (Eph. 4:26-27; Psa. 60:1; 78:50).

6. Teach them it is all right to say "No" to requests, and that this is not selfish (Matt. 5:37; James 5:12).

7. Encourage them verbally — encourage them to mend broken relationships (Matt. 5:23-24; 18:15-17; Eph. 4:29). Be positive with them during difficult times. Help them to see that the differences

they have compared to other people is part of their unique identity given to them by God.

8. Teach them to take risks; that failure might occur, but they can learn from it (Matt. 14:25-30).

9. Teach them to put their esteem in Christ and not in others (Matt. 11:28-30). Accept them for who they are (Rom. 15:7). This might be the most important ingredient to helping their self-esteem. Teach them they have dignity and worth.

10. Be loving and confrontive with inappropriate behaviors and thoughts (Matt. 14:31; John 20:29-31). Paul wrote in 1 Thessalonians 2:11-12, "For you know that we dealt with each of you as a father deals with his own children, encouraging, comforting and urging you to live lives worthy of God, who calls you into his kingdom and glory."

11. Spend time with them (Luke 19:5-6; John 4:40).

12. Do nice things for them, and surprise them (1 John 3:17-18). Giving gifts for no reason is an excellent way to build a person's self-esteem. They may tell you "Oh, you shouldn't have." Keep giving them gifts anyway. Giving gifts to others is a blessing (Acts 20:35). Jesus gave to others, so should we (John 3:16).

13. Be gentle with people in their time of need (Matt. 11:29; 1 Thess. 2:7). Become Jesus to them (Eph. 5:1-2).

We have seen the wonderful wisdom contained in Scripture on how to improve our esteem, as well as others. In the last chapter, we will take an in-depth look at the names and titles that describe Christians.

Notes

1. Bruce Parmenter, *What the Bible Says about Self-Esteem*, p. 145.

2. Alfred Adler, *The Practice and Theory of Individual Psychology* (London: Routledge & Kegan Paul, Ltd., 1923), p. 3.

3. *Family Circle*, March 12, 1996, p. 108.

4. Kaz Cooke, *Real Gorgeous: The Truth about Body and Beauty* (New York: W.W. Norton and Co., 1996), p. 140.

11 Names and Titles the Bible Gives to God's People

In one of Josh McDowell's books, he observes that a healthy self-image is "seeing ourselves as God sees us — no more and no less."[1] Many people have difficulty accepting how God sees them. They know what God says about them, but they think it is too good to be true. These people can only see the negative in themselves. The problem is they have lost their biblical balance about the nature of man. The fact is that God is delighted with his people. Zephaniah 3:17 says he takes delight in us, rejoices over us with singing. Many other verses speak of God being delighted (Deut. 30:9; Psa. 35:27; 149:4; Isa. 42:1; 62:4; 65:19; Micah 1:16; Matt. 12:18). Zephaniah 3:19 tells us that God gives us praise and honor.

Many people have an esteem vertigo problem. Vertigo is a condition where a person feels a dizzy, whirling sensation and might lose balance. Painful events tend to knock the esteem out of balance, putting it in a tailspin. Some pilots can experience vertigo and lose their orientation to which direction they are going. This is why pilots must depend on their instrument panel. When our esteem goes into a tailspin, we need an instrument panel. The best instrument panel for correct self-esteem is the Bible.

Romans 12:3 directs us to have sober judgment of ourselves. What does this mean? The word "sober" here means to be in sound mind. Many people have developed an esteem that is from a futile mind (Eph. 4:17). Too many Christians today are measuring their esteem the way the non-Christian world measures theirs. Since Christians have the mind of Christ (1 Cor. 2:16), our esteem should come from the mind of Christ and not the world's.

While I was waiting for a boarding pass in an airport, a man in a nice three-piece suit cut in front of about 20 people. He told the ticket agent he needed a boarding pass and could not wait with us. The ticket agent told him he needed to go back to the end of the line. At this the man said, "Do you know who I am?" The ticket agent then grabbed the microphone and asked for security, saying, "There is a man here who does not know who he is." Did this man really not know who he was? Do we really know who we are?

Socrates said, *gnowthi seauton* – "Know thyself." This inscription is over the Temple of Delphi. Self-knowledge and self-acceptance are important parts of a healthy self-esteem. It is also important to be known by God to build a healthy self-esteem. David knew himself and he also knew that he was known by God. David writes in Psalm 139:1-4, "O Lord, you have searched me and you know me. You know when I sit and when I rise; you perceive my thoughts from afar. You discern my going out and my lying down; you are familiar with all my ways. Before a word is on my tongue you know it completely, O Lord."

David writes in Psalm 139:13-14, "For you created my inmost being; you knit me together in my mother's womb. I praise you because I am fearfully and wonderfully made; your works are wonderful, I know that full well." What did David mean when he said, "I know it full well"? He is saying that he knows who he is in the image of God. He is also saying that he accepts who he is in the image of God. This "knowledge" is a wonderful gift. Remember in the previous chapter, I wrote that David had the best self-esteem of any person mentioned in the Bible. It is from this verse that I gain this belief.

One of my favorite verses about self-esteem is Ecclesiastes 3:11. It states, "He has made everything beautiful in its time. He has also set eternity in the hearts of men; yet they cannot fathom what God has done from the beginning to end." Why do people have a difficult time "fathoming" what God has done and the beauty of his creation, including man? It is because God sees man in a way that man thinks is too good to be true. This is why God states in Isaiah 55:8, "For my thoughts are not your thoughts, neither are your ways my ways." Too many times we look at ourselves from a "worldly" point of view. Paul writes in 2 Corinthians 5:16, "So from now on we regard no one from a worldly point of view. Though we once regarded Christ in this way, we do so no longer."

Name changes in Scripture occurred at least five times. The names were changed to reflect the personality attributes.

Genesis 17:1-8 — Abram to Abraham which means "father of many."

Genesis 17:15 — Sarai to Sarah which means "Princess."

Genesis 35:10 — Jacob to Israel which means "he struggles with God."

Matthew 16:13-19 — Simon to Peter which means "rock."

Acts 4:36 — Joseph to Barnabas which means "Son of Encouragement."

Other names already reflect the individual and there was no reason to change them. Some examples are: **David** — *beloved*; **Ezekiel** — *God is strong*; **Elisha** — *God is Savior*; **Gideon** — *great warrior*; **Isaiah** — *salvation of the Lord*; **Lazarus** — *God has helped*; **Adam** — *red earth*; **Esther** — *star*; **Ruth** — *something worth seeing*; **Matthew** — *gift of the Lord*; and **Luke** — *light giving*.

The names and titles that God gave these people reflected who they were. This does not mean that all names and their meanings in the Bible show the true person, nature or essence. For example, Caleb means "dog"; Deborah means "bee"; Leah means "cow." On the other hand many of the names in Scripture tell about a person's nature. For example, Timothy means "Worshiper of God" and Peter means "rock or stone." Bruce Parmenter wrote, "The believer does not derive his self-esteem from culture, from his self-estimate, or from what others say about him. He derives his self-esteem from what God has said about him and from what God does for him."[2]

In 2 Corinthians 5:16 Paul wrote, "So from now on we regard no one from a worldly point of view. Though we once regarded Christ in this way, we do so no longer." If Paul did not regard people from a worldly point of view, his new viewpoint had to be Godly. In this day and age, the world's point of view of the self and life is a lot more popular than the Godly point of view. This should not be! It is important to take on a Godly point of view of self and life.

Paul wrote in Philippians 2:5, "Your attitude should be the same as that of Christ Jesus." Paul did not give us specific areas on which to concentrate, so it must be that all of our attitudes must be in agreement with Christ (2 Cor. 10:5). The *American College Dictionary* defines attitude as, "position, disposition, or manner with regard to a person or thing." So our position on the subject of self and self-esteem must be the same as Christ Jesus, or be in obedience to Christ. This attitude will be reflected in the names a person calls themselves.

Our Many New Names

What's in a name really? Well if the "name" is found in Scripture, this is where a Christian can gain his or her identity. Paul wrote that our name is from God. In Ephesians 3:14-15 Paul wrote, "For this reason I kneel before the Father, from whom his whole family in heaven and on earth derives its name." The word "derives" means "to come from."

The Bible teaches that God shall give people new names. Isaiah 62:2 states, "The nations will see your righteousness, and all kings your glory; you will be called by a new name that the mouth of the Lord will bestow." Acts 11:26 states, "And when he found him, he brought him to Antioch. So for a whole year Barnabas and Saul met with the church and taught great numbers of people. The disciples were first called Christians at Antioch." The word "bestow" is translated in the King James Version as "name." The word occurs in Psalm 3:3; 31:39; Isaiah 45:4; 61:3; 62:2; and Jeremiah 23:2.

Paul wrote in 1 Corinthians 15:10, "But by the grace of God I am what I am, and his grace to me was not without effect." He understood his identity came from God. God also changed his name from Saul to Paul; thus giving him a fresh start (Acts 13:9). What names or titles do Christians derive from God that show their spiritual nature? The one I want to begin with is "Blood-Bought Princes and Princesses of Christ." Many verses in the Bible teach about Christians being bought by the blood of Christ. Some of them are Revelation 1:7; 14:4; Ephesians 1:7; 1 Corinthians 6:19-20; Psalm 74:2 and 1 Peter 1:18-19.

Some of the other names that are given Christians according to Scripture are:

➢ *Salt of the earth* – Matthew 5:13. Salt has three major purposes:
1. seasoning
2. preservative
3. healing of infection

➢ *Light of the world* – Matthew 5:14-16 (Heb. 1:7; 1 Thess. 5:5). Light is needed only in darkness. Light is now also being used in communication. As light of the world, we should communicate the gospel to the darkness.

➢ *Bruised and smoldering wicks* – Matthew 12:20. God wants to heal us and set us ablaze again.

➢ *Princes or princesses* – Matthew 27:11. Jesus is claiming to be a King. This would make us royalty since we are co-heirs with Jesus (Rom. 8:17). Isaiah 49:7 declares, "This is what the LORD says – the Redeemer and Holy One of Israel – to him who was despised and abhorred by the nations, to the servant of rulers: 'Kings will see you and rise up, princes will see and bow down, because of the Lord, who is faithful, the Holy One of Israel, who has chosen you'." Kings only rise for royalty!

The idea that Christians are princesses and princes is an inferred interpretation. The Bible describes God as King in many passages. Some of them are: Jeremiah 10:10; Psalm 10:16; 24:7-10; 29:10; 44:4; 47:7; 84:3; 95:3; 145:1; Zephaniah 3:15; Zechariah 14:9; 1 Timothy 1:17; 6:15; Revelation 15:3. Since God is King, and we are his children (John 1:12) and have been grafted into his kingdom (Rom. 11:17); and have been adopted by the King and have become heirs (Gal. 4:6-7; Rom. 8:15-17) we are princes and princesses.

➢ *Children of God* – John 1:12; 1 John 3:1-2. First John 3:1 reads, "How great is the love the Father has lavished on us, that we should be called children of God! And that is what we are! . . ." John 1:12 says that God gave us the "right to become children of God" (Rom. 8:16-17, 21).

➢ *New creations* – 2 Corinthians 5:17; Galatians 6:15. It is important you realize who you are in the image of God; but also who you are in the re-creation of Christ.

➢ *Ambassadors* – 2 Corinthians 5:20. We are a people through whom God makes his appeal.

➢ *Righteousness* – 2 Corinthians 5:21. We are the righteousness of God because of the death of Jesus.

➢ *Crucified with Christ* – Galatians 2:20. We are a people in whom Christ lives. We are a people that God loves.

➢ *Precious, honored, loved and exchangeable* – Isaiah 43:4. Jesus was our exchange at Calvary (2 Cor. 5:21). David recognized he was precious to God (Psa. 22:20; 35:17). David writes that our blood is precious to God (Psa. 72:14). Our blood is precious because it is our life (Lev. 17:11, 14). So our life is precious to God. David even writes that precious is the death of the saints to God (Psa. 116:15).

➢ *God's witnesses. Chosen servants* – Isaiah 43:10.

➢ *God's people* – Isaiah 51:16.

➢ *Beloved of the Lord* – Deuteronomy 33:12.

➢ *People who bear the name of Jesus, Christians* – Acts 11:26; 1 Peter 4:16 (1 Pet. 4:14)

➢ *Unforgettable, engraved on the palm of God's hand* – Isaiah 49:15-16. We are always before God.

> *The only reason the angels rejoice* — Luke 15:7, 10.

> *New, created to be like God in true righteousness and holiness* — Ephesians 4:24.

> *Blessed in the heavenly realm with every spiritual blessing in Christ* — Ephesians 1:3.

> *Complete, given the fullness of Christ* — Colossians 2:10.

> *The apple of God's eye* — Zechariah 2:8; Deuteronomy 32:10; Psalm 17:8.

> *Loved with an everlasting love from God* — Jeremiah 31:3; Romans 1:7.

> *God's elect, strangers in the world* — 1 Peter 1:1. Chosen to be sanctified by the spirit. We have been sprinkled by Jesus' blood.

> *Enemies of the devil* — 1 Peter 5:8.

> *Made by God* — Psalm 100:3. We belong to God, we are his sheep (Isa. 43:1).

> *Knit together by God, fearfully and wonderfully made* — Psalm 139:13-14. This idea can be fully known by man.

> *Chosen by God, his treasured possession* — Deuteronomy 7:6. (Isa. 43:1; 1 Pet. 1:20)

> *Strangers in this world* — 1 Peter 1:1, 17; 2:11.

> *Good soldiers that should not be entangled by civilian affairs* — 2 Timothy 2:3-4.

> *A people God listens to* — Isaiah 65:24, Joshua 10:14. God will meet our needs even before we ask.

> *The reason Jesus chose to die* — Matthew 26:52-53.

> *Made holy by the sacrifice of Jesus Christ* — Hebrews 10:10.

> *Forgiven, purified from all sin and all unrighteousness* — 1 John 1:7–2:2.

> *A branch from the vine (Jesus)* — John 15:5.

> *Formed by God, for God, to praise God* — Isaiah 43:21.

> *A kingdom and priests to serve God* — Revelation 1:6.

> *Members of the body of Christ* — 1 Corinthians 12:27; Ephesians 5:30.

> *Chosen, holy, dearly loved* — Colossians 3:12. "Chosen" is one of my favorite titles that God gives us. It means that he selected us, or picked us (Isa. 43:2).

➤ *Chosen, holy and blameless in his sight* – Ephesians 1:4.

➤ *Redeemed by the precious blood of Jesus* – 1 Peter 1:18-19 (Psa. 107:2; Eph. 1:7; Rev. 14:3).

➤ *Chosen people, royal priests, holy nation, belonging to God, praise declarers* – 1 Peter 2:9-10.

➤ *Blameless* – Philippians 2:15 (Rev. 14:5). Pure, children of God, without fault.

➤ *Friends of Jesus* – John 15:13-15. Valuable enough that Jesus would die for us willingly (John 10:18; Matt. 26:53-54)

➤ *Chosen* – John 15:16; Colossians 3:12; 1 Thess. 1:4. Deuteronomy 7:7-8 states, "The Lord did not set his affection on you and choose you because you were more numerous than other people, for you were the fewest of all peoples. But it was because the Lord loved you and kept the oath he swore to your forefathers that he brought you out with a mighty hand and redeemed you from the land of slavery, from the power of Pharaoh king of Egypt." Paul wrote in Romans 11:5, "So too, at the present time there is a remnant chosen by grace."

➤ *Sheep that know the Shepherd (Jesus)* – John 10:11, 14. The Shepherd also knows the sheep.

➤ *Saints often oppressed by the devil* – Romans 1:7, Daniel 7:25; Revelation 13:10.

➤ *Slaves to righteousness* – Romans 6:18.

➤ *Not condemned* – Romans 8:1.

➤ *God's children* – Romans 8:16-17. Heirs of God and co-heirs with Christ.

➤ *More than conquerors through Christ who loves us* – Romans 8:37.

➤ *Sons of God* – Romans 8:14-15; Galatians 3:26; 4:6. Leviticus 26:9 states, "I will look on you with favor and make you fruitful and increase your numbers, and I will keep my covenant with you." Does God have his favorite people? I prefer what Paul wrote in Galatians 4:5, "to redeem those under law, that we might receive the full rights of sons." It is my belief that Christians have more rights and privileges in God's sight. Psalm 4:3 reminds us, "Know that the Lord has set apart the godly for himself; the Lord will hear when I call to him." The Hebrew word for "set apart" means to distinguish. The Greek word for "set apart" means to do wonderful things for. This is an absolutely wonderful verse!

All of the people on the earth are of equal value in the sight of God. John 3:16 states it best, "For God so loved the world, that he gave his only Son." This verse states that God loves everyone. The Bible teaches that God is not a respecter of persons, nor does he show favoritism (Acts 10:34; Deut. 10:17; 2 Chron. 19:7; Job 34:19; Rom. 2:11; Gal. 2:6; Col. 3:25; 1 Pet. 1:17). The Bible also teaches that God causes rain to fall on the just and the unjust (Matt. 5:45).

Jesus does refer to some people as dogs and pigs in Matthew 7:6. This verse states, "Do not give dogs what is sacred, do not throw your pearls before pigs. If you do, they may trample them under their feet, and then turn and tear you to pieces." I believe that the dogs and pigs Jesus is referring to are people who are not yet ready to receive the gospel. The Bible states that God grants favors (Psa. 90:17; Isa. 26:12; Neh. 5:19; 13:31; Ezek. 32:19). Granting favors to certain people is not the same as having favorites!

➢ *Belonging to Christ, heirs according to the promise. Abraham's seed* — Galatians 3:29.

➢ *God's workmanship, created to do good works that God prepared in advance for us to do* — Ephesians 2:10.

➢ *Friends of God* — 1 John 4:1, 7, 11.

➢ *In this world we are like him* — 1 John 4:17.

➢ *The people of his pasture, under his care* — Psalm 95:7.

➢ *Adopted as sons and daughters* — Ephesians 1:5. The Greek word *huiothesia* is the word for adoption. Literally translated it means "placing a son." In the King James Version of the Bible it occurs 5 times (Rom. 8:15, 23; 9:4; Gal. 4:5; Eph. 1:5). This word is only used by Paul. The word signifies the place, condition or position of a son given to someone to whom it does not naturally belong. It is important for Christians to realize that they have been adopted into the family of God. This is one of the ways that Satan will lose his power.

➤ *Ministers of a new covenant* – 2 Corinthians 3:6.

➤ *The temple of God, place God's Spirit lives* – 1 Corinthians 3:16. Thomas Carlyle said, "There is one temple in the universe – the human body. We touch heaven when we touch the human body." Henry Drummond said, "Do we carry about with us a sense of God? Do we carry the thought of Him with us wherever we go? If not, we have missed the greatest part of life. Do we have the feeling and conviction of God's abiding presence wherever we go?"

➤ *God's fellow workers, God's field, God's building* – 1 Corinthians 3:9.

➤ *Of Christ* – 1 Corinthians 3:23.

➤ *Temple of the Holy Spirit, owned by God* – 1 Corinthians 6:19.

➤ *Bought at a price* – 1 Corinthians 6:20; 7:23. Exodus 15:16 says, "terror and dread will fall upon them. By the power of your arm they will be as still as a stone – until the people you bought pass by." The price that God paid for us was Jesus' death at Calvary! Revelation 14:4 states, "They follow the Lamb wherever he goes. They were purchased from among men and offered as first-fruits to God and the Lamb." (See Psa. 74:2.) Matthew 13:44-46 describes us as treasure hidden in a field or fine pearls of great value that God sold all he had to buy (Rev. 17:14).

➤ *Brothers (and sisters) to other Christians who are responsible to God* – 1 Corinthians 7:24.

➤ *Washed, sanctified, and justified in the name of the Lord Jesus Christ and by the Spirit of our God* – 1 Corinthians 6:11.

➤ *Can be infants in Christ and worldly* – 1 Corinthians 3:1, 3.

➤ *Servants of God* – 1 Chronicles 6:49; 2 Chronicles 24:9; Nehemiah 10:29; Daniel 9:11; Titus 1:1; James 1:1; Revelation 15:3.

➤ *Servants of Christ* – 1 Corinthians 3:5; 4:1; Galatians 1:10; Colossians 4:12; Romans 1:1; Jude 1:1.

➤ *Christians are a people who will live with Christ, reign for ever and ever* – 2 Timothy 2:11; Revelation 22:5.

➤ *Crowned by God* – Isaiah 62:3; Psalm 103:4; Zechariah 9:16.

➤ *Attractive and beautiful* – Zechariah 9:17.

➤ *Accepted by Christ* – Romans 15:7.

➤ *Adopted into royalty* – Romans 8:15; Galatians 4:4-7.

➤ *Circumcised by Christ to put off the sinful nature or flesh* – Colossians 2:11.

➤ *Made a little lower than the heavenly beings or God* – Psalm 8:5. We are crowned with glory and honor.

➤ *Rulers over the work of God's hands* – Psalm 8:6. God has put everything under our feet.

➤ *A people God cares for and about* – 1 Peter 5:7.

➤ *Children of God* – 1 John 4:4.

➤ *Equal to all Christians* – Matthew 20:12.

➤ *Loved by God* – 1 John 4:10-11.

➤ *God lives in us* – 1 John 4:12.

➤ *Sacred, God's holy temple* – 1 Corinthians 3:17.

➤ *Servants of Christ who have been entrusted with the secret things of God* – 1 Corinthians 4:1.

➤ *From God and he listens to us* – 1 John 4:6.

➤ *A people that have 10,000 guardians in Christ* – 1 Corinthians 4:14.

➤ *Redeemed under the law; we have been given full rights as sons* – Galatians 4:5.

➤ *The world is not worthy of us!* – Hebrews 11:37-38.

➤ *Clay in the hands of the master potter* – Jeremiah 18:3-6 states, "So I went down to the potter's house, and I saw him working at the wheel. But the pot he was shaping from the clay was marred in his hands; so the potter formed it into another pot, shaping it as seemed best to him. Then the word of the Lord came to me: 'O house of Israel, can I not do with you as this potter does?' declares the Lord. 'Like clay in the hand of the potter, so are you in my hand, O house of Israel.'"

As we close this book, it is vitally important to take the teachings and insights gained here and apply them to your everyday life. One of the best ways to do this begins with daily prayer and Bible study (Josh. 1:8-9). It would be good to pray as David did in Psalm 86:11-13. It would be great if we just took the Bible, God, and Jesus at their word. We need to believe the titles that God has given us as his children. We need to fully believe what the Bible teaches us about a Christ-centered esteem. When we don't, we are calling God, Jesus, the Holy Spirit, and the Bible liars!

Notes

1. Josh McDowell, *His Image . . . My Image*, p. 31.
2. Bruce Parmenter, *What the Bible Says about Self-Esteem*, p. 102.

Select Bibliography

Adler, Alfred. *The Practice and Theory of Individual Psychology.* London: Routledge & Kegan Paul, Ltd., 1923.

Anderson, Neil and Steve Russo. *The Seduction of Our Children.* Eugene: Harvest House, 1991.

Bernard, Harold W. *Human Development in Western Culture.* 5th Edition. Boston: Allyn and Bacon, 1978.

Bruder, Ernest E. *Ministering to Deeply Troubled People.* Englewood Cliffs, NJ: Prentice-Hall, 1963.

Cooke, Kaz. *Real Gorgeous: The Truth about Body and Beauty.* New York: W.W. Norton and Co., 1996.

Dobson, James. *Hide and Seek.* Old Tappan, NJ: Revell, 1974.

Fiensy, David A. *New Testament Introduction.* Joplin, MO: College Press, 1994.

Gardner, Richard A. *Self-Esteem Problems of Children.* Cresskill, NJ: Creative Therapeutics, 1992.

George, Bob. *Classic Christianity.* Eugene: Harvest House, 1989.

Gill, James. "Indispensible Self-Esteem." In *Human Development,* Vol. 1, 1980.

Hadfield, J.A. *Psychology and Morals*. New York: R.N. McBride and Co., 1936.

Hyder, O. Quentin. *The Christian's Handbook of Psychiatry*. Old Tappan, NJ: Revell, 1971.

Johnston, Joni. *Learning to Love the Way You Look*. Deerfield Beach, FL: Health Communications, 1994.

Katz, Barney and Louis P. Thorpe. *The Psychology of Abnormal Behavior*. The Ronald Press, 1948.

Leman, Kevin. *The Pleasers*. Old Tappan, NJ: Revell, 1987.

Lewis, C.S. *Screwtape Letters*. New York: MacMillan, 1943.

May, Rolo. *Psychology and Human Dilemma*. New York: Van Nostrand Reinhold, 1967.

McDowell, Josh. *His Image . . . My Image*. San Bernardino, CA: Here's Life, 1984.

McGee, Robert S. *The Search for Significance*. Houston: Rapha, 1990.

McGinnis, Alan Loy. *The Friendship Factor*. Minneapolis: Augsburg, 1979.

_____ . *Confidence — How to Succeed at Being Yourself*. Minneapolis: Augsburg, 1987.

Menninger, Karl. *The Vital Balance*. New York: Viking Press, 1963.

Missildine, W. Hugh. *Your Inner Child of the Past*. New York: Simon and Schuster, 1963.

Muedeking, George H. *Emotional Problems and the Bible*. Philadelphia: Muhlenberg Press, 1956.

O'Conner, Elizabeth. *Search for Silence*. Waco, TX: Word, 1972.

Olson, G. Keith. *Why Teenagers Act the Way They Do*. Loveland, CO: Group, 1987.

Parker, William R. and Elaine St. John. *Prayer Can Change Your Life*. Englewood Cliffs, NJ: Prentice-Hall, 1956.

Parmenter, Bruce. *What the Bible Says About Self-Esteem*. Joplin: College Press, 1986.

Rainey, Dennis and Barbara. *Building Your Mate's Self-Esteem*. San Bernardino, CA: Here's Life, 1990.

Seamonds. David. *Healing for Damaged Emotions.* Wheaton, IL: Victor, 1981.

Schuller, Robert H. *Self-Esteem the New Reformation.* Waco: Word, 1982.

Skogland, Elizabeth. *The Whole Christian.* New York: Harper and Row, 1976.

Smalley, Gary. *Hidden Keys of a Loving Lasting Marriage.* Grand Rapids: Zondervan, 1984.

——————. *The Blessing.* Nashville: Nelson, 1986.

Stafford, Tim. *Love, Sex and the Whole Person.* Grand Rapids: Zondervan, 1991.

Tally, Jim and Bobbie Reed. *Too Close Too Soon.* Nashville: Thomas Nelson, 1982.

Thomas, Clayton L. Ed. *Taber's Cyclopedic Medical Dictionary.* Philadelphia: F.A. Davis Co., 1993.

Waitley, Denis. *Seeds of Greatness.* Old Tappan, NJ: Revell, 1983.

Wright, H. Norman. *Improving Your Self-Image.* Eugene: Harvest House, 1983.

Ziglar, Zig. *See You at the Top.* Gretna, LA: Pelican, 1979.